Secrets
to
Share

Compiled by
Pat Edwards and
Wendy Body

Fife Council Education Department
King's Road Primary School
King's Crescent, Rosyth KY11 2RS

Acknowledgements

We are grateful to the following for permission to reproduce copyright material: The Bodley Head on behalf of the author for an extract from *Seal Secret* by Aidan Chambers; The Bodley Head on behalf of the author and Scholastic Inc for 'Forgetful Fred' from *The Practical Princess and Other Liberating Fairy Tales* by Jay Williams, Copyright © 1978 by Jay Williams; William Collins Sons & Co Ltd for an extract from *The Secret in the Attic* by Carolyn Keene; Heinemann Publishers Australia Pty Ltd for 'Things in the Jungle' from *Shadow Among the Leaves* by Bill Scott; Scholastic-TAB Publications Ltd for 'Strange Journey or Strange Dream' from *The Seventh Princess* by Nick Sullivan © 1983 by Nick Sullivan (pub Scholastic-TAB Publications Ltd). Pages 50-1 were written by Bill Boyle.

We are grateful to the following for permission to reproduce photographs: Camera Press, page 51 *below left* (Steve Benbow); Celtic Picture Agency page 51 *above* (Frank Greaves), 51 *below right* (Barry Webb); Tim Graham Picture Library, pages 55 *below*, 56, 57 *below*; Frank Lane Picture Agency, page 39; Rie Munoz, Alaskan Artist, © 1984, Rie Munoz, Alaska Northwest Publishing Company, page 94; Rex Features, page 57 *above*; Photosource, pages 54, 55 *above*; Royal National Eisteddfod of Wales, page 51 *centre*; Seaphot, page 38 (David Rootes).

Illustrators, other than those acknowledged with each story, include: John Fairbridge pp.4-5; Kim Robert pp.28-9; Bruce Lachlan pp.34-5; Bettina Guthridge pp.36-7; Paul Collicutt pp.50-1 and pp.95-6; Liz McLennan pp.52-3; Jocelyn Bell p.63; Sandra Laroche p.79; Deborah Savin pp.80-1.

Contents

What was in Pandora's box?

All the troubles in the world! At least, that's the way the story goes.

According to the Greek myth, Pandora was a beautiful girl, the fairest in all the world. She was created specially because Zeus, king of the gods, wanted revenge on the people of the earth. For Prometheus had interfered in Zeus' plans by stealing fire from the gods and giving it to the people on earth. Zeus was furious and ordered that Prometheus be bound with unbreakable chains to a high mountain peak, and stay there forever with an eagle endlessly tearing at his belly and eating his liver.

Next Zeus planned his revenge on the people of the earth, for now that they had fire, they had become much too much like the gods for his comfort. He decided to create a beautiful woman, and invited all the gods to give her something special.

The gods showered Pandora with beautiful gifts, but there were also two that were dangerous. Hermes, the messenger, gave her a beautiful golden box, but told her she must never, never open it. Hera, wife to Zeus, gave Pandora curiosity.

Hermes took Pandora to Epimetheus, brother of Prometheus, saying that Pandora was to be his wife. Epimetheus and Pandora were married and all went well to begin with. However, thanks to Hera, Pandora was curious and she could not resist opening the golden box. As soon as she did, out flew a swarming, biting, scratching horde of horrible creatures. Their names were Sickness, Old Age, Hunger, Poverty and Despair. They were all the ills that bring pain, sorrow and death.

So Zeus got his revenge — or almost. For one of the creatures was Hope, and Hope has helped people to live with all the others.

Today, when someone speaks of a Pandora's box, she or he usually means a present which seems to be valuable, but is really something from which great and unexpected troubles come.

CZAR TROJAN'S EARS

Characters

FIRST STORYTELLER	PRIME MINISTER
SECOND STORYTELLER	SHEPHERD
CZAR TROJAN	FLUTE (a voice only)
VANEK, the barber's assistant	CHILDREN (as many as you like)

SETTING: A room in the Czar's palace.

SCENE   1

(*The curtain is down. First storyteller comes on from left and bows.*)

FIRST STORYTELLER: Once upon a time, long ago and far away, there lived a Czar named Trojan. Now Trojan had a strange secret. He had the ears of a goat. He kept them hidden beneath a very tall crown, specially made, for he hated the thought that the people of the town would laugh at him behind his back.

(*Second storyteller comes on from right.*)

SECOND STORYTELLER: For that's what people often do you know, when someone is strange or different. But let me tell the next bit. Czar Trojan could keep his head covered in front of everyone (for he was the greatest in the land) except his barber. Even a mighty Czar cannot stop his hair from growing.

6

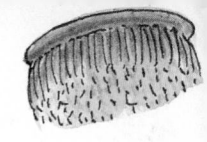
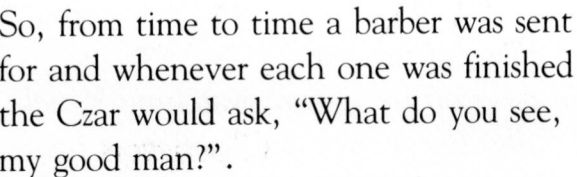

So, from time to time a barber was sent for and whenever each one was finished the Czar would ask, "What do you see, my good man?".

FIRST STORYTELLER: And the barbers, being honest men, would answer, "The Czar has the ears of a goat".

SECOND STORYTELLER: Which, of course, was the wrong thing to say, for as soon as the Czar heard that, he would immediately cut off the barber's head.

(*First storyteller draws a finger across his or her throat.*)

FIRST STORYTELLER:
And snip, snip, snum.
His life was done.

SECOND STORYTELLER: The Czar had almost run out of barbers, when one day . . .

FIRST STORYTELLER: But why not come to the palace with us and see what happened?

(*The curtain is drawn up. First storyteller walks left, second storyteller walks right. We see the Czar sitting on his throne. He is frowning at a young man who is standing before him.*)

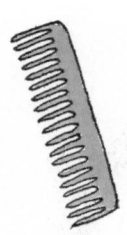

CZAR TROJAN: You look very young to be a barber. I expected someone much older.

VANEK: True it is, Sire, that I am not yet a barber, but my master says I am a very able assistant. He, alas, is ill today, so he sent me in his place.

CZAR TROJAN: Hmm . . . well, let us see
        what you can do, barber's assistant. You
        may cut my hair.

(*He takes off his crown, watching Vanek
carefully. But Vanek does not show his
surprise.*)

VANEK: A little bit off the top and sides, Sire?

CZAR TROJAN: Yes, and be careful not to
        snip too close to my ears.

(*Vanek begins to cut the Czar's hair.*)

VANEK: Nice weather we're having, Sire.

CZAR TROJAN: Hmm . . . Tell me barber's
        assistant, what do you see?

VANEK: I see that my Czar has fine, dark,
        thick hair.

(*He cuts some more.*)

CZAR TROJAN: And have you noticed
        anything about my head, barber's assistant?

(*Vanek stands back and looks carefully.*)

VANEK: Well, Sire, perhaps you are getting
        a little thin on top, but I wouldn't
        worry about it.

(*Vanek finishes the haircut and hands the
Czar a mirror.*)

CZAR TROJAN: Excellent, excellent! But
        one thing more. Do you notice anything
        strange about my ears?

VANEK: (*looking surprised*) About your
        ears, Sire?

    CZAR TROJAN: Yes, my ears!

    VANEK: Why no, I can't say I have.
            (*He pauses.*) Except . . .

    CZAR TROJAN: Yes? Out with it!

VANEK: Well, they are very nice ears, if I may say so.

CZAR TROJAN: (*smiling happily*) Yes, you may say so, barber's assistant. Call at the Prime Minister's office on your way out and collect twelve gold ducats. And from now on you may come to the palace on the first day of every month to cut my hair.

VANEK: (*bowing deeply*) Why, thank you, Sire. (*The curtain falls. Vanek steps out from behind it and speaks directly to the audience.*)

VANEK: Well, how about that for a stroke of luck? I couldn't tell him that my master sent me because he'd heard every barber who went to the palace met with an unfortunate accident. He lost his head! Now I know why. The Czar doesn't want anyone to know about those ears of his. And imagine — twelve gold ducats (*he jingles the money*) every month just for cutting his hair. Provided I keep my mouth shut, of course. Well, that's easily done. His secret is safe. No one will ever know from me that Czar Trojan has the ears of a goat. (*He goes off whistling.*)

FIRST STORYTELLER: But it's hard to keep a secret, especially if you're a barber.
Will Vanek hold his tongue?

SECOND STORYTELLER:
Snip, snip, snout
We'll soon find out.
(*They go off.*)

SCENE 2

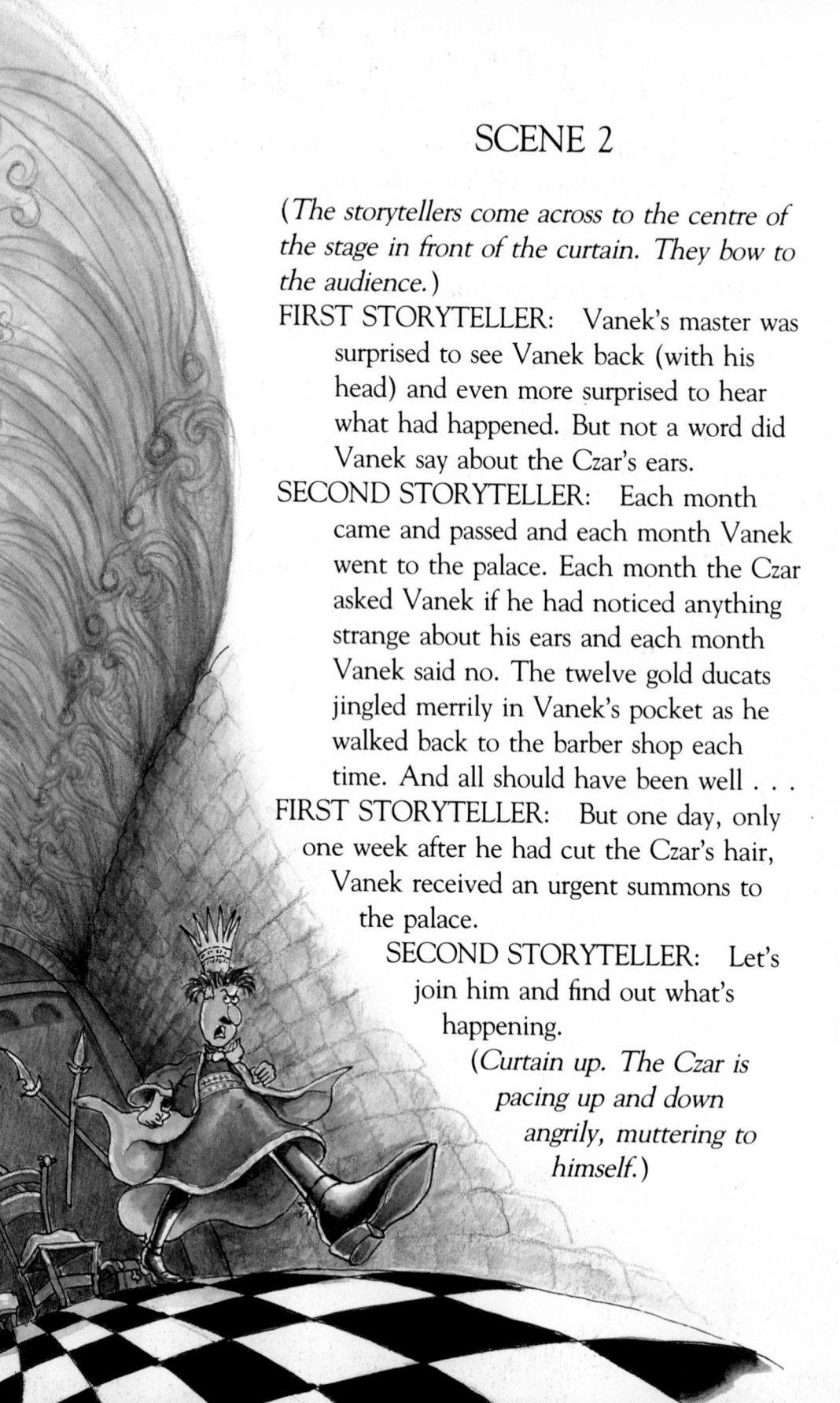

(*The storytellers come across to the centre of the stage in front of the curtain. They bow to the audience.*)

FIRST STORYTELLER: Vanek's master was surprised to see Vanek back (with his head) and even more surprised to hear what had happened. But not a word did Vanek say about the Czar's ears.

SECOND STORYTELLER: Each month came and passed and each month Vanek went to the palace. Each month the Czar asked Vanek if he had noticed anything strange about his ears and each month Vanek said no. The twelve gold ducats jingled merrily in Vanek's pocket as he walked back to the barber shop each time. And all should have been well . . .

FIRST STORYTELLER: But one day, only one week after he had cut the Czar's hair, Vanek received an urgent summons to the palace.

SECOND STORYTELLER: Let's join him and find out what's happening.

(*Curtain up. The Czar is pacing up and down angrily, muttering to himself.*)

CZAR TROJAN: That miserable little tattle-tale! That horrible little sneak. That vile secret-sharer! I'll make him pay!

(*The Prime Minister enters, dragging Vanek by the ear. He gives him a shove that sends Vanek sprawling at the Czar's feet.*)

PRIME MINISTER: The barber's assistant is here, Sire.

CZAR TROJAN: Oh wretched worm of a barber's assistant! How dare you tell tales about me around the town!

VANEK: (*getting to his knees*) But, Sire, I swear I didn't.

CZAR TROJAN: Prime Minister, tell this contemptible little gossip what I heard while walking in the garden this morning.

PRIME MINISTER: The Czar heard some children singing the most dreadful song on the other side of the palace wall.

CZAR TROJAN: Sing it, Prime Minster. After all, you heard it too.

PRIME MINISTER: I can hardly bear to do so, Sire.

CZAR TROJAN: (*angrily*) Sing!

PRIME MINISTER: (*clearing his throat*) Ahem! (*sings*)
Who has a crown and a velvet coat?
Who has the hairy ears of a goat?
Czar Trojan has, Czar Trojan has,
Czar Trojan has the ears of a goat.

(*He is very embarrassed.*) I'm not sure about the tune, Sire.

CZAR TROJAN: Oh, fiddle the tune!
     Just bring me my sword.
  Prepare to lose your head, you detestable bearer of tales.
VANEK: (*who has been listening with horror*) Oh, Sire, Sire,
     hear me I pray! I vow I have not told your secret to a
     living soul. I beg of you. Ask the children who told them
     of your ears. They cannot say it was I.
CZAR TROJAN: Oh, very well. But only so no one can say
     I am not a just and honourable ruler. Prime Minister, find
     out from the children who told them about my ears.
PRIME MINISTER: At once, Sire. (*He goes off.*)
FIRST STORYTELLER: And so, while the Czar paced up and
     down and Vanek shook like a jelly, the Prime Minister
     went down into the town to find the children. A great
     deal of time went by.
SECOND STORYTELLER: Tick-tock, tick-tock!
FIRST STORYTELLER: The Czar grew even angrier —
     though it did not seem possible that he could, and Vanek
     began to say his prayers. And still more time went by.
SECOND STORYTELLER: Tick-tock, tick-tock!
FIRST STORYTELLER: The Czar got sore feet and sat
     down and Vanek finished his prayers and began to wonder
     if the Czar would let him eat some lunch before his head
     was cut off. Then . . .

12

(*The Prime Minister enters with a shepherd.*)

CZAR TROJAN: (*springing to his feet*) About time! Where have you been and who is this?

PRIME MINISTER: Forgive me, Sire, but such a tale I've been told I hardly know where to start.

CZAR TROJAN: Start by telling me why you bring back someone who looks like a shepherd when I sent you to talk to children.

PRIME MINISTER: He's the end of the story, Sire. Or, no, perhaps he's the beginning.

CZAR TROJAN: Oh, get on with it or I'll be here all night.

PRIME MINISTER: Well, Sire, when I asked the children who taught them their song, one of them said she made it up from something she heard her mother telling a neighbour. I questioned the mother, who said she got it from her husband, who heard it from the baker who said the butcher told him . . .

CZAR TROJAN: So the whole town knows?

PRIME MINISTER: It seems so, Sire. After I'd questioned the candlestick maker and the school teacher and the doctor and the dentist and the . . .

CZAR TROJAN: (*interrupting*) All right, all right, hurry it up!

PRIME MINISTER: At last I came to this shepherd.

CZAR TROJAN: Finally, we're getting somewhere at last.

VANEK: (*jumping to his feet*) But I never saw him
in my life!

CZAR TROJAN: Back on your knees villain and hold
your tongue! Now shepherd, speak out and speak
truthfully. Who told you I had the ears of a goat?
Was it this gossiping little toad of a barber's assistant?

SHEPHERD: No, Sire. My flute did.

ALL: (*together*) Your flute?

SHEPHERD: My flute. Listen. (*He lifts it to
his lips and blows.*)

FLUTE VOICE: (*It's really someone off stage.*)
Who has a crown and a velvet coat?
Who has the hairy ears of a goat?
Czar Trojan has, Czar Trojan has,
Czar Trojan has the ears of a goat!

CZAR TROJAN: This is magic! Or is it some clever trick?

SHEPHERD: Oh no, Sire. Try it yourself. (*He hands the
flute to the Czar.*) Now put it to your lips and blow.

(*Czar Trojan does this. All listen, amazed.*)

FLUTE VOICE:
Who has a crown and a velvet coat?
Who has the hairy ears of a goat?
Czar Trojan has, Czar Trojan has,
Czar Trojan has the ears of a goat.

CZAR TROJAN: (*gazing at the flute in wonder*) Truly
magic! Where did you get this flute?

SHEPHERD: I made it a week ago from a branch I cut
from an elder tree.

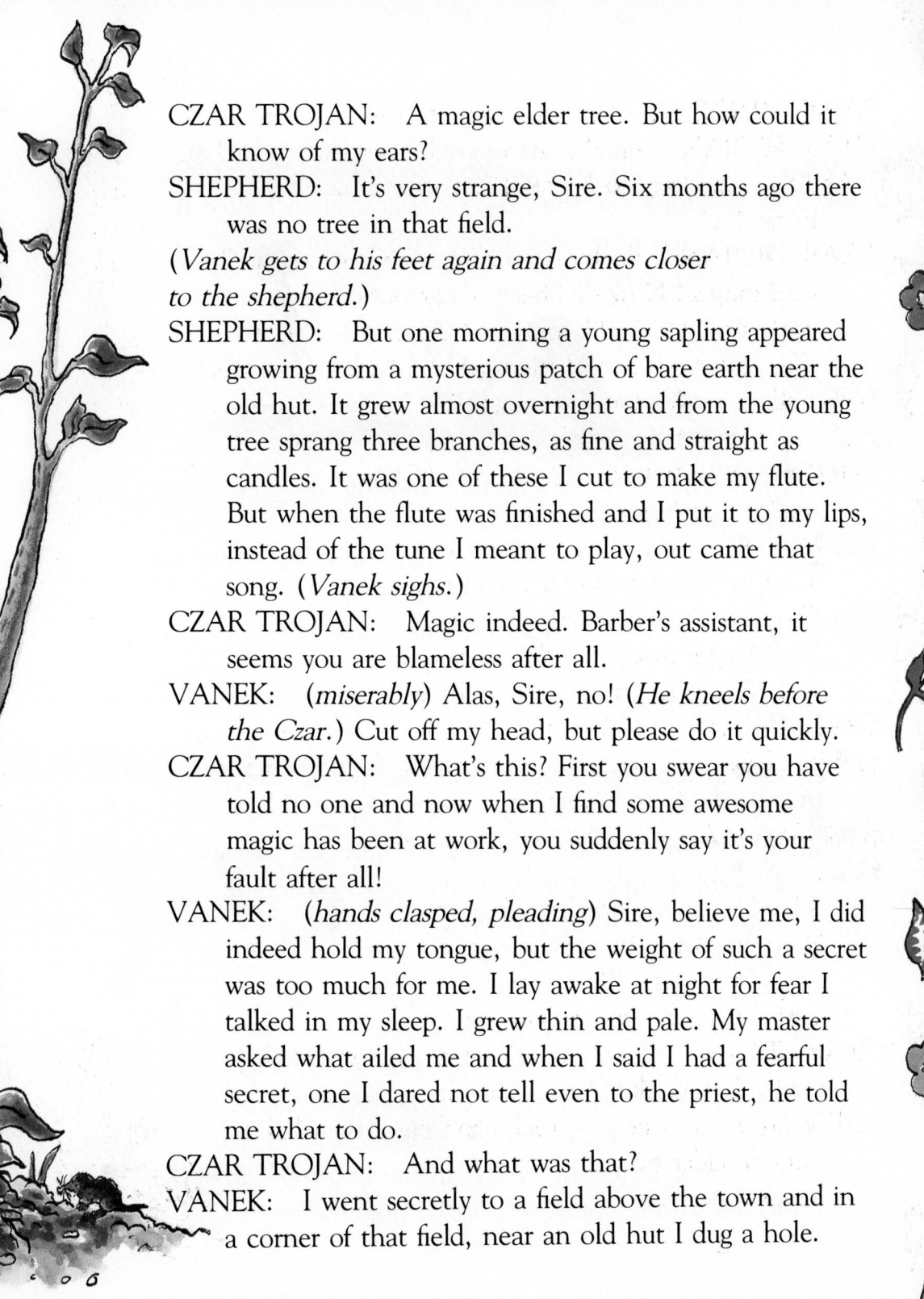

CZAR TROJAN: A magic elder tree. But how could it know of my ears?

SHEPHERD: It's very strange, Sire. Six months ago there was no tree in that field.

(*Vanek gets to his feet again and comes closer to the shepherd.*)

SHEPHERD: But one morning a young sapling appeared growing from a mysterious patch of bare earth near the old hut. It grew almost overnight and from the young tree sprang three branches, as fine and straight as candles. It was one of these I cut to make my flute. But when the flute was finished and I put it to my lips, instead of the tune I meant to play, out came that song. (*Vanek sighs.*)

CZAR TROJAN: Magic indeed. Barber's assistant, it seems you are blameless after all.

VANEK: (*miserably*) Alas, Sire, no! (*He kneels before the Czar.*) Cut off my head, but please do it quickly.

CZAR TROJAN: What's this? First you swear you have told no one and now when I find some awesome magic has been at work, you suddenly say it's your fault after all!

VANEK: (*hands clasped, pleading*) Sire, believe me, I did indeed hold my tongue, but the weight of such a secret was too much for me. I lay awake at night for fear I talked in my sleep. I grew thin and pale. My master asked what ailed me and when I said I had a fearful secret, one I dared not tell even to the priest, he told me what to do.

CZAR TROJAN: And what was that?

VANEK: I went secretly to a field above the town and in a corner of that field, near an old hut I dug a hole.

SHEPHERD: So that's why there was a mysterious bare patch!

VANEK: I put my head in the hole and said three times, "Czar Trojan has the ears of a goat". Then I filled the hole in and went back home with a light heart and merry feet.

PRIME MINISTER: (*excitedly*) And the tree grew from the earth that knew the secret.

CZAR TROJAN: (*thoughtfully*) And from the tree came the flute.

VANEK: (*sadly*) And from the flute came the song.

SHEPHERD: The song that I played in the market place for all to hear.

VANEK: (*even more sadly*) So you see, Sire, I am guilty. Would you mind making sure your sword is very sharp before starting. (*He bows his head.*)

CZAR TROJAN: No one can say I am not a just and honourable ruler. On your feet barber's assistant. You need have no fear for your head.

PRIME MINISTER: Shall I send soldiers to cut down the tree, Sire?

CZAR TROJAN: No, Prime Minister.
Leave it where it stands. That tree was sent to prove to me that truth will be out, that no secret can be kept for ever. It's no use blaming each other when a secret is spilt for the very branches of a tree can sing it to the world. Come, it must be time for lunch.

(*The Czar, Prime Minister, Vanek and the shepherd all exit.*)

FIRST STORYTELLER: (*moving across the centre stage as the others leave*) And so from that time onward the people of the town knew their Czar had the ears of a goat, but none cared for he was a just and honourable ruler.

SECOND STORYTELLER: (*also moving across to centre stage*) The shepherd went back to his field, leaving the magic flute with the Czar, who never played it, and Vanek continued to cut the Czar's hair every month and every month he took home twelve ducats of gold.

FIRST STORYTELLER: But down in the village the children still sang their song. Listen, there it is now . . .

(*As the curtain falls, children's voices are heard from the back of the hall.*)

    CHILDREN: (*singing*)

      Who has a crown and a velvet coat?
      Who has the hairy ears of a goat?
      Czar Trojan has, Czar Trojan has,
      Czar Trojan has the ears of a goat.

    SECOND STORYTELLER:

      What's left to say but –
      Snip, snip, snum.

    FIRST STORYTELLER:

      That's all there is;
      Our play is done.

    (*They bow and go off.*)

Adapted by Pat Edwards from the Hungarian folktale *Czar Trojan's Ears*. Illustrated by Bucket.

Things in the Jungle

Does the land have secrets? Is there a spirit-world around us, of which we are seldom aware?

Jo (Josephine) Brady can't explain the feelings she gets when she has to ride through the vine-tangled jungle some distance from her home . . .

Jo's father, Sam Brady, owned the farm furthest up the main valley toward the mountains. The soil was poorer and stonier than the rich loamy flats downstream. Sam had taken the contract for the mail-run and the school bus to help support himself and his family. Mrs Nichols only left the old inn about once a month and she never went further than the Village. She was the only one living between Sam's farm and the foot of the main range, and he delivered her mail once a week. At least, Jo did it for him. Because he was a country man and a friendly man he also brought up the old lady's few requirements for her; fresh bread and fresh meat. Each Saturday morning Jo would sling the few stores in bags across the saddle behind her, stow the mail in her pocket and set off to visit the old lady.

Not that the old lady got much mail. She got letters from a sister and a brother-in-law in Sydney, and sometimes letters in long brown-paper envelopes with the letters OHMS on them. This Saturday there was one of these letters, as well as the groceries, so Jo began getting ready.

"Bother it all!" she thought as she dressed in jeans, a T-shirt and a long-sleeved shirt against the thorns of the wait-a-whiles. "I'd rather go down to Valley Harbour with Mum, Dad and Paul! Mrs Nichols is a nice old thing, but I don't like having the same job every week. I suppose I wouldn't mind so much if it wasn't for 'Them'."

She always thought of the things that hid in the vine-tangled jungle as Them. A year ago, just after her eleventh birthday, she had tried to tell her parents about her fears. They hadn't taken much notice. Her father had ridden up with her one Saturday on his big bay gelding to make sure she was all right, that was all. They hadn't come near the bridle-track that day, trust Them! That night he had said to her, "Jo, it's perfectly safe. You can't get lost, all you have to do is follow the track. It's not that far either. You can ride through the scrub in half an hour. You're a big girl now. I know I can trust you not to do anything silly like leaving the path. Anyway, even if you did get off the track all you have to do is ride downhill till you cut across it again. It follows the creek all the way."

"I know all that," she had grumbled unhappily.

"Well, don't be a selfish girl," said Sam. "People in the country have to help each other. Now, let's hear no more about it!"

Jo knew that this was going to be a bad day as soon as she got to the boundary fence. She climbed down from Bessie's saddle and looped the reins over her arm. The slip-rail post was held upright by a ring of stiff wire and she had to edge it gradually up and over the top of the sapling holding the sliprail. At last she forced it over the shiny wood, put the wires on the ground and led Bessie through. She hung the bridle over a fence-post. She would like to have left the wires down until she came back but there were cows in the paddock and she couldn't take the chance of them getting through. They would wander off along the edge of the jungle, especially old Pansy who was very cunning at opening gates and escaping.

That was why her father had made the wire bow holding the rails so tight. She had a struggle to slip the toe of the sapling back into the toe-hold of the anchor post. At last she had the wires taut enough to loop the top wire again. She was puffing when she remounted.

Jo turned Bessie's head to the bridle-path that led into the jungle, then reined her to a standstill. It was going to be bad. A wind blew briskly, stirring the matted tangle of the tree-tops. That meant They would be out. They were always stirred up when there was a strong wind. She wouldn't be able to hear Them as she travelled along the path because of the wind-song through the branches, falling leaves, and the chafe and rustle of twigs. They would be able to get close to her without her being able to hear Them! She shivered a little, and gooseflesh stood out in tiny hummocks on her arms. For a moment she thought of going home again but she knew she couldn't do that. There were the things to take Mrs Nichols, and anyway, what would her father say? Sam was a good man, and a kind one, but he was very stern about things he said were your "duty". How could she explain it to him? Especially when it was only a feeling she had. She had never actually seen one of Them. She sighed and gathered up the reins, urging Bessie toward the faint opening in the thickets of lantana which marked the beginning of the bridle-path.

Bessie plodded slowly along. She would never go fast when she was going away from home. Jo felt quite angry with her, and thought she might stop and get a switch from a tree to urge the fat old mare along. She had to duck her head down beside the warm brown neck as they entered the jungle. She couldn't feel any breeze when they got among the towering trunks, but she could hear the stir far above and a small litter of twigs and leaves fell as Bessie plodded her dawdling way down the slope to the creek-bank where the first crossing shone faintly in the green gloom. The track crossed and re-crossed the creek all the way through the jungle to avoid spurs of rock or tangled thickets on one bank or the other. Jo felt that They weren't there yet, but she knew that somewhere ahead They would be waiting. They would follow behind, and rustle through the forest on either side of the track. They would be overhead, peering down. They were too fast to be seen. When They looked at her it was always when she was staring in another direction. The minute she moved her head They would slip away out of sight behind tree trunks. It was an eerie feeling. Today, so far, They had not come. She always knew when They did. The skin would prickle on the back of her neck and a nasty kind of thrill would run right through her body and not go away. There was no mistaking the feeling.

It was at the fourth crossing of the creek that They came. Bessie had tottered down the drop of the bank and was wading across the gravel bar when Jo suddenly knew They were there. They were in the trees above her, and she shuddered as she rode up the far slope and back under the canopy. High above her the leaves stirred, the branches swayed and the vines waved gently, swinging from the branches like huge pythons. Jo urged Bessie with her knees and tried to watch the tree-tops over the path ahead, but she could see nothing. Once she thought she caught a glimpse of something dark and diamond-shaped but it vanished quickly and she wasn't sure she'd really seen it or if her eyes were playing tricks. It looked a bit like something she had seen on the television at school; a film about the Great Barrier Reef. A thing called a manta ray. The woman on the television had said they grew to enormous size. Some of them could weigh up to a tonne! But manta rays lived in the sea and the sea was sixty kilometres away. It couldn't be flying round in the tops of the trees. Jo urged Bessie forward again, but the stubborn old mare refused to quicken her steady plod. Jo wished she'd broken off a switch before she came into the jungle, but she certainly wasn't going to get down and get one now.

They were getting bolder by the time she reached the sixth crossing of the creek. She was about three-parts through now, and starting to feel a little desperate. Bessie seemed to sense her fear. She snorted and stepped out faster. They were crowding thickly above her now, she could feel Them! A great wind seemed to be troubling the leaves and the thick vines swayed violently. She set her mouth in a firm line. Despite her resolve to be brave, she felt tears begin to sting behind her eyes. Fear froze her throat, making it hard to breathe, but she kept on.

Suddenly, without warning, They were gone. Though nothing had changed outwardly, all at once she felt the way she did when she had been in a storm and come through the door of the kitchen at home, to the warmth of the wood stove and the baking and cooking smells that meant safety and security.

Then, gradually, this feeling of peace also began to be disturbed. Something was still following her, out of sight and completely silent. Whatever it was she knew it to be even more dreadful than the tormentors who had gone away. Then ahead through the great thick trunks of the trees she saw the brighter light that meant the ending of the jungle patch. In a moment she and Bessie had broken through the thick growth of stinging trees and lantana marking the edge of the scrub. They were safely at the foot of the rocky slope leading up to the old inn. She could see the tall figure of Mrs Nichols waiting for her on the porch of the square building with the tumble-down stables at the back almost covered with rambling trumpet-vine. She was safe.

Bess blew hard through her nostrils and began the stiff climb up the hill. She knew she had reached the end of her outward journey. Now she could laze in the shade for a while.

Mrs Nichols waved one arm to Jo and went into the inn. The kettle would be boiling and tea made before Jo got off her mare. They always had a cup of tea before she went home. Home! With a shudder she realised that soon, quite soon, she would have to go through the forest again! She closed her eyes and swore softly, using a word she had learned from Junie Christie whose father owned the picture show. Jo didn't know what it meant, but it made her feel better. She dug her heels into Bessie's flanks and hurried the lazy mare uphill as fast as she would go. When she got there she dismounted and slung the reins over an old iron hook buried deeply in the trunk of the spreading fig-tree close to the inn. She unslung the bags of groceries, carrying them over her shoulder up the three steps and on to the little porch.

There was a small table ready set with cups, sugar bowl and bread-and-butter plates. Two straight-backed wooden chairs were pulled up to the table. Jo lowered the groceries to the floor and waited. In a minute Mrs Nichols came through the thick heavy door carrying a small tray with a fat brown teapot and a plate of scones.

"Sit down, Josephine," she said. She put the tray on the table and looked hard at her visitor. "What's the matter with you? You look upset."

Jo tried to smile, but found she couldn't. Suddenly she found herself telling the old lady all about Them. She hadn't ever meant to tell anyone in case they thought she was going crazy and laughed at her, but after the strain of her ride it all burst out. Mrs Nichols didn't laugh. She watched Jo with her big soft brown eyes and waited with a serious face until Jo had finished speaking. The girl was almost in tears as she ended the story. Mrs Nichols nodded quietly.

"So they are still there," she said, almost as if she was speaking to herself. Then she smiled at Jo. "I'm going to tell you something, but you must keep the secret. The ones you call Them, those are things from the very old times. They don't really belong around here. They used to live further south, but when all the trees got cut down and chopped up they came up here to live. They had another proper name, but when I was told about them people called them 'Flats'. That's what they look like. They're big and square and very thin through. They don't catch human beings, they feed on little bandicoots and rabbits. One rabbit a year is enough for them. They hide on a branch and when the rabbit is under them, they drop down and wrap themselves around it, and that's the way they eat."

"But what are they?" asked Jo, fascinated.

"Nobody knows properly these days. The Aboriginal people had a name for them, their right name, but that's all lost now. But they still know about them. My grandmother told me. I've never seen one, but I heard about them from her when I was a little girl. There are some things you don't forget."

"How did your grandmother know?"

"Ah, well, she was an Aborigine, though she married a white man. My mother married a white man, too. Dad was a carpenter at Woolloomooloo in Sydney. But it was Grannie who told me those things. She came to live with us after Grandad died. That's how I heard about the Flats. Though I didn't know there were any left around the place. I didn't know where they might have gone, but I thought they'd all gone away."

"Mrs Nichols, what was that other thing? Those — Flats — they went away very fast when it came along. I think they must have been frightened of it. But it didn't hurt me, or chase the Flats or anything. It just came along behind me. I even felt happier when it was there."

Mrs Nichols looked grimly at her. "Ah, now, that's something I do know about. That thing really belongs here. This is its home; the place where it has always lived. Remember I told you once that Aborigines didn't come here much? Well, you're a girl, and almost a woman, so I can tell you. Men never came here, only women. Once a year when a little flower came out in the grass down at the beach, the old women would know the time had come. You know your father's farm? Well, the men would come along that far to protect the women, but they couldn't go past it, they had to camp there. The old women would come up here with all the young girls that had grown up in the last year. They'd have a ceremony here."

"What ceremony? What did they do?"

"You don't need to know that. Now, that thing is called an old name, but the English word for it is the Follower. Nobody has ever seen it, it always sneaks up from behind. It's very strong. No wonder the Flats ran away, they'd be frightened of it. It doesn't travel about much, and it doesn't mind women, but it creeps up behind the men sometimes if they're thinking bad things, and nobody sees them again."

Jo sipped her black sweet tea. It was nearly cold, she had been so interested in the story she had forgotten all about it. She thought for a minute. Was the old lady telling her a ghost story just to frighten her? She looked at the wrinkled brown face with the soft eyes that regarded her across the table, and decided that even if it was only a story, Mrs Nichols really believed it. "If it doesn't mind women, why was it following me then?"

"Maybe the Follower heard the Flats making a noise, and it woke up and went to see what they were doing. Those Flats, they're tricky, they might chase you for fun, but they'd go away fast if that thing came. They'd be more frightened of it than you were of them!"

"It was really spooky. I was scared," said Jo slowly.

"Well, you would be. They're strong, some of those old things. But I'll tell you what. There's something you can do. Have you got anything with you that's red? The Follower likes red. In the old times, the women used to bring it red flowers, berries, seeds — all things like that. Then it would like them and keep them safe."

Jo thought for a moment. "There's my hanky," she said, pulling a bit of crimson cloth from the pocket of her jeans. It was a new one she had got from her pen-friend in Adelaide for Christmas, one of a set of three — green, gold and crimson. She had brought the red one with her this day. "Might this do?"

"It's bright enough," said Mrs Nichols. "Yes, I think it'd do. Now, do you remember where you were when the Flats went away and the Follower came?"

Jo nodded.

"Well, hang that hanky on a wait-a-while there and leave it. Then it'll know you're a friend and it won't bother you. It might even look after you."

"I hope it does," said Jo feelingly. "If it just keeps that other lot away from me I'd be happy."

"You never know, it might. Pour yourself another cup of tea, love. Yes, it might be friendly. You'd always be safe through there if it was. There's nothing else around here that would be game to touch you if the Follower was your friend."

"Did your grandmother tell you about the Follower too?"

"Yes, when I married Nichols and we were coming to live up here. You see, old Mister Nichols had two sons, my husband and his brother, David. When he died he left the old place here to my husband, and the land where the rainforest is he left to David. But David's a carpenter in Sydney, and he didn't want to come up here to live, so he stayed down there. He still owns the land. That's why nothing was ever done to clear and farm it. He's got a good business down there, he doesn't need the money. He says he likes to think of it staying the way it was when they were boys and used to play in there."

"I can understand that, I think," said Jo.

"When we were married and I told Grannie we were coming here to live, she told me about the Follower. Her people used to live round here, that's how she knew. I didn't think about it much then. When you're young, you think the old ones don't know much and are superstitious. But when I'd lived here for a long time, specially since Nichols died, I've felt the Follower about and that's how I knew it was true. But I never told anyone before because they'd laugh and say I was dotty. I only told you because you felt it was there."

Jo nodded thoughtfully. It was true she'd felt it. It was also true she wouldn't be game to tell anyone else about it in case they thought she was dotty too! But it was a relief to know she had someone she could talk to now. She smiled at Mrs Nichols and nodded. It was good, too, that it was someone she loved and trusted. "I'm so glad you told me," she said. "I don't mind nearly so much now I know about it. I'll leave the hanky where you said. It can't do any harm, anyway."

Mrs Nichols smiled back at her and then leaned across the table and patted the back of her hand. "Those old people lived here for a long time, Jo. They knew a lot that's been lost in the last hundred years."

"Did the Follower ever catch any men while you've been here?"

"I've never heard about it if it did. There was a story Nichols used to tell, about his grandfather being blamed for a prospector who disappeared, but men often died in those days, with no roads or anything. It all blew over, anyway. Now I'll get my grocery list for your father to give Mr Johnson at the store. It's nearly time you were starting back."

When Jo reached the place in the rainforest where the Follower had been, she stopped and took the little, hemmed square of red cloth from her pocket and hung it carefully on a wait-a-while frond beside the track. She made sure it was firmly hooked on the cruel thorns and couldn't be blown away, then prepared to ride on. But she suddenly felt she should do something more, so she spoke aloud: "This is a present for you. I hope you like it, it came all the way from Adelaide!"

She felt silly to be sitting there on the mare's back talking to nothing. If anyone heard her they would think she was crazy! Still, there could be no harm in it, and after she started Bessie along the track again she felt strangely warmed and comforted. The jungle didn't seem nearly so frightening now. Anyway, Bess was going faster, as she always did when you turned her head for home. Even the thought of the Flats didn't bother her much any more, now she knew about them. Jo began to sing softly as she rode.

Bill Scott   Illustrated by John Fairbridge

CRACK the

Do you like reading stories or watching films about spies? From time to time, the spies have to send off messages in secret code. Have you ever wondered who first thought of using numbers and symbols in this way?

20-8-5-25,
13-21-19-20,
2-5,
16-12-15-20-20-9-14-7,
19-15-13-5-20-8-9-14-7,
13-25-19-20-5-18-9-15-21-19.

8-5-18-5,
9-19,
1-14,
9-14-22-9-20-1-20-9-15-14
20-15,
13-25,
2-9-18-20-8-4-1-25,
16-1-18-20-20-25.

Check with an encyclopaedia and it will probably tell you that the first codes we have real information about are the ones used by Italian rulers around the beginning of the fifteenth century. At first they were very simple, but they soon became very complicated and before long all the European governments were using them when they wanted to send secret information.

A nice easy code for beginning code-writers is the one shown on the next page. Here each letter of the alphabet is given a number. The speech bubbles on these pages all use this code.

CODE

C=3 O=15 D=4 E=5

9,
19-16-25,
23-9-20-8,
13-25,
12-9-20-20-12-5,
5-25-5,
19-15-13-5-20-8-9-14-7,
2-5-7-9-14-14-9-14-7,
23-9-20-8,
6.

a	b	c	d	e	f	g	h	i
1	2	3	4	5	6	7	8	9

j	k	l	m	n	o	p	q	r
10	11	12	13	14	15	16	17	18

s	t	u	v	w	x	y	z
19	20	21	22	23	24	25	26

It's a good idea to put a comma after each word in your message

7-5-5,
20-8-1-14-11-19,
1,
2-15-20.

Of course, you can number backwards by starting at z, and calling that letter 1 so that a ends up as 26. Or you could start with f or n or s — or wherever you like!

Some codes substitute letters, others use symbols, e.g.

a = z   or   a = ∅
b = y   b = ϙ
c = x   c = ⅄
d = w   d = Σ

All you have to do is pick your code and hey presto! You, too, can hand on secret messages.

1-8-1,
19-16-9-5-19,
1-20,
23-15-18-11.

The Secret of the Old Attic

Solving mysteries is Nancy Drew's speciality. This time she is set on a mysterious trail, by elderly Mr March, to find some missing music. Mr March's son, Fipp, had died on a training mission as a soldier. Fipp had been a talented musician. He had written some very fine unpublished songs. Before leaving home, Fipp had hidden his music. Mr March desperately wants to find and sell the music. He needs the money to look after his grandchild Susan. Nancy has come to Mr March's old mansion to track down the music. Strange things have been happening. Effie, the maid, saw a man sneaking away from the house in the middle of the night and Nancy had discovered his footprints circling the house. Nancy wants to search the old attic for clues ...

Nancy set the candle in a holder. She left the kitchen, went to the second floor, and stopped at the foot of the attic stairway. There she touched a match to the wick and held the candle high in her hand as she ascended cautiously. Just as she reached the top of the steps, the light went out.

Nancy's heart began to pound. Was someone up there? She shook off her momentary fear.

"It was only a draught from that leaky window," Nancy told herself. She struck an extra match and relighted the wick.

Nancy stepped into the attic. The candle flickered again and nearly went out. Something moved.

"My own shadow, of course," she reasoned. "But how grotesque I look!"

Nancy's eyes focused on a massive wardrobe which stood against the far wall.

"I'll search that first," she decided, crossing the attic.

Setting the candle on the floor, she grasped the knob of the door and pulled.

"Wonder what I'll find?" she asked herself.

The door did not give. At the same moment there was a creaking sound. Nancy could not tell where it had come from. She picked up the candle and looked around.

"It's nothing, I'm sure," Nancy told herself, but she could not shake off the uneasy feeling that had come over her.

Once more she put down the candle and tugged at the door. It gave suddenly, swinging outward on a squeaky hinge.

From within, a long bony arm reached out towards Nancy's throat!

It was impossible for Nancy to stifle a scream as the long bony fingers brushed against her throat. She staggered backwards. The candlelight flickered wildly.

"Come away! Come away before that — that thing gets you!" shrieked someone behind her.

The voice was Effie's. The maid, worried about Nancy, had followed her to the attic.

"It's nothing. Nothing but a skeleton," said Nancy, her own voice a trifle unsteady.

"It struck you with its bony hand!" quavered Effie. "Oh, I'm getting out of this house tonight, and I'm never coming back!" she announced, starting down the steps.

"Please don't go downstairs and frighten Susan," Nancy pleaded, her own momentary fear gone. "Surely you see what happened?"

"You were attacked by a skeleton!"

"No, Effie. The thing is hanging inside the wardrobe. One hand seems to be attached to a nail on the door. When I jerked it open, the arm swung out and the fingers brushed me."

Nancy reached into the closet and touched the chalk-coloured bones.

"What's a thing like that doing here, anyway?" Effie asked, in a voice less shaky than before. "I don't like it!"

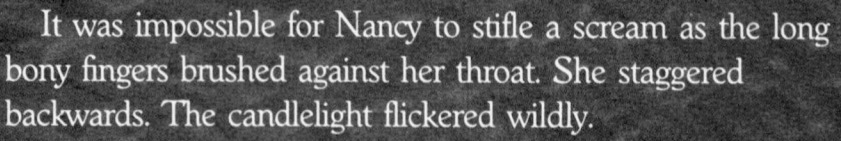

Before Nancy could reply, they heard footsteps on the attic stairs. Mr March called, "Anything wrong up there? I heard someone scream."

"We found a skeleton in the wardrobe," Nancy explained. "It startled us."

Mr March slowly climbed to the attic and went towards the open wardrobe.

"Oh *that!*" he said in relief. "I'd forgotten all about it. Fact is, I didn't know Fipp had put it in the wardrobe."

The elderly man then explained that the skeleton originally had been brought there by a young medical student, a cousin of Fipp's.

"You know how boys are," he added with a chuckle. "They used this skeleton on Halloween, and never did take it away."

"You're sure your son put it here?" Nancy asked thoughtfully.

"Who else could have done it?"

Nancy did not reply. Instead she began an investigation of the wardrobe. She figured it was just possible Fipp March had rigged the strange figure to frighten away all but members of his own family.

Perhaps this was his hiding place for the missing music!

Excited, Nancy held up the candle in order to examine every inch of the old piece of furniture. When a hasty glance revealed nothing but dust and cobwebs, she tapped the sides, top, and bottom for sliding panels. None came to light.

Effie, tired of waiting, coaxed Nancy to go downstairs. Mr March, concerned about Susan during their long absence, said he thought they should all go below. Nancy did not want to give up the search, but out of deference to the elderly man's wishes, she reluctantly followed the others to the second floor.

"I'm going to look at that old wardrobe again soon," she said to herself. "I have a hunch it holds a strange secret."

Caroyln Keene
Illustrated by Peter Foster   33

HOLD YOUR BREATH!

Sleuthing, or detecting, can be scary work. And when you're scared, often you gasp or hold your breath. Have you ever said "I held my breath to see what would happen next"?

Of course you only do it for a few seconds. Holding your breath for too long can harm your body.

What's so important about breathing?

Well, that's the way your body gets the oxygen it needs for all those cells you have. Your body is made up of many millions of tiny cells. These cells need oxygen. Without it, they die. Five minutes is the most you can live without oxygen.

How does your body get oxygen to its cells?

When you breathe in, you take oxygen into your lungs. The oxygen in your lungs goes into your bloodstream and your bloodstream carries the oxygen to the millions of tiny cells in your body. During their work of keeping you alive and healthy, these cells make carbon dioxide. Too much carbon dioxide is bad for you so your blood takes it off, back to your lungs and, when you breathe out, you breathe out the carbon dioxide.

Oxygen (which you need) in. Carbon dioxide (which you don't need) out. Neat trick, eh?

Normally you don't have to think about breathing. Your body does it automatically because you have a kind of "remote control" in your brain. This "reads" how much carbon dioxide is travelling in your blood. Too much? "Breathe out" goes the order. Oxygen needed? "Breathe in" goes the order, and you take a deep breath.

So what happens when you hold your breath?

- Without oxygen your cells can't do their work. You start to feel weak and dizzy. You might even faint.
- Your face gets red because too much carbon dioxide in your blood makes your small blood vessels get bigger, so more of the red colour of blood can be seen through your skin.

BUT don't worry, your body just won't let you hold your breath for too long. It will force you to breathe — to keep you alive!

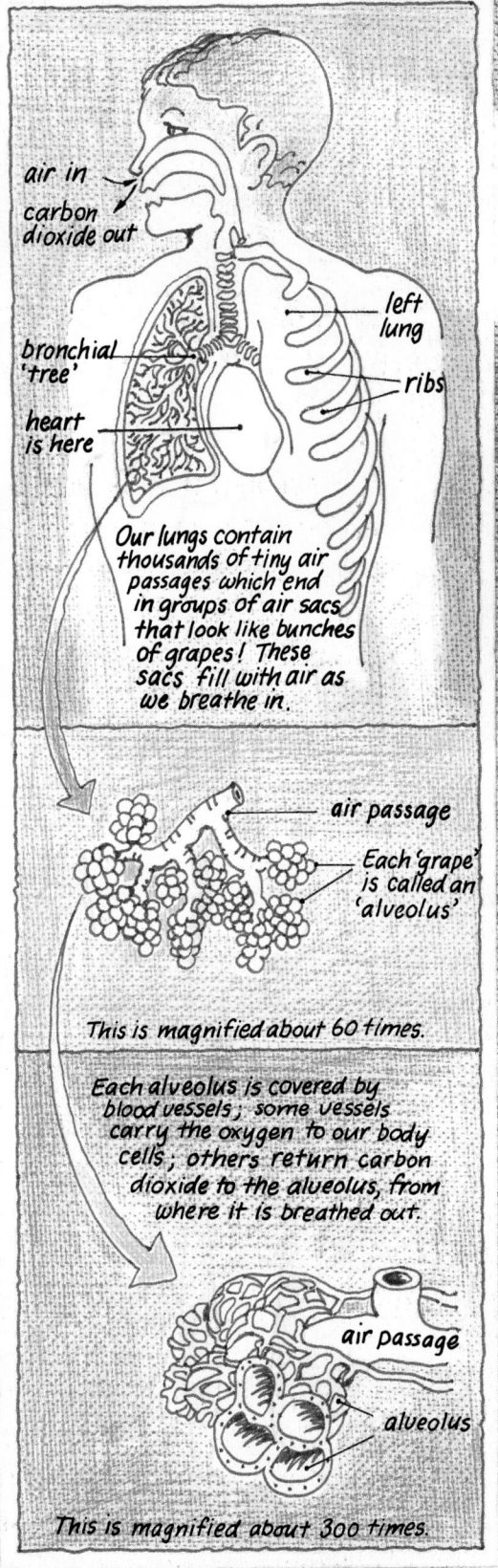

air in
carbon dioxide out

left lung

bronchial 'tree'

ribs

heart is here

Our lungs contain thousands of tiny air passages which end in groups of air sacs that look like bunches of grapes! These sacs fill with air as we breathe in.

air passage

Each 'grape' is called an 'alveolus'

This is magnified about 60 times.

Each alveolus is covered by blood vessels; some vessels carry the oxygen to our body cells; others return carbon dioxide to the alveolus, from where it is breathed out.

air passage

alveolus

This is magnified about 300 times.

A sleuth needs a nose

Ever been called a 'nosey parker'?

Sniff! sniff!

Has anyone ever said to you, 'Follow your nose and you'll find it'?

Phrases like *sniffing out, follow your nose*, and *nosey parker* have come about because people through the ages have discovered that noses are wonderful tools that constantly give us news reports about the world.

Detectives don't really sniff out the clues. They use their eyes more than anything. They are always looking for tiny details, ones that may not seem important at first glance, but just might turn out to be the vital clues needed to solve a mystery. The phrase was probably used for people after someone noticed a tracker dog sniffing its way along a trail.

Everyone follows their nose, of course! You can't help it! But nosey parkers are people who 'poke their noses' into other people's business. It can also mean someone who is very curious — just like a good detective.

36

What about that nose of yours?

Whatever its shape or size, it's special, just to you. And you can't get along without using it for breathing — most of the time, anyway.

The most interesting thing your nose does for you is pick up thousands of different smells. How does it do this?

Deep inside there's an *olfactory region*, which is packed with special 'smelling nerves'. Just one sniff of air can bring you all sorts of clues about the place you're in at that moment.

Dogs have a particularly keen sense of smell. A dog can follow a trail hours after it has been made. It can even follow it in total darkness as clearly as a human can follow a road in broad daylight.

The noses of many species of bat have very sensitive skin folds that help these bats to pick up echoes of the sound waves they send out. That way they can detect flying insects and also avoid bumping into obstacles.

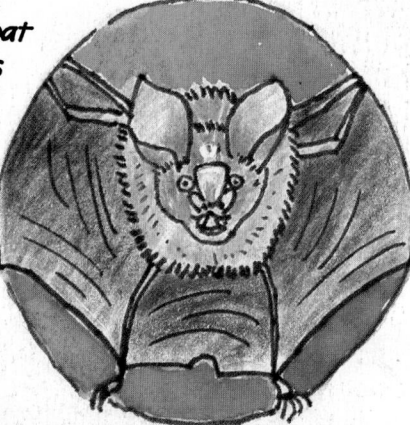

Camels' noses have small slits that can close to keep out dust and sand.

Seals can close their noses when diving.

FACTS FOR NOSEY PARKERS.

A pig uses its nose to dig for food.
And we all know what elephants do with theirs!

Seals

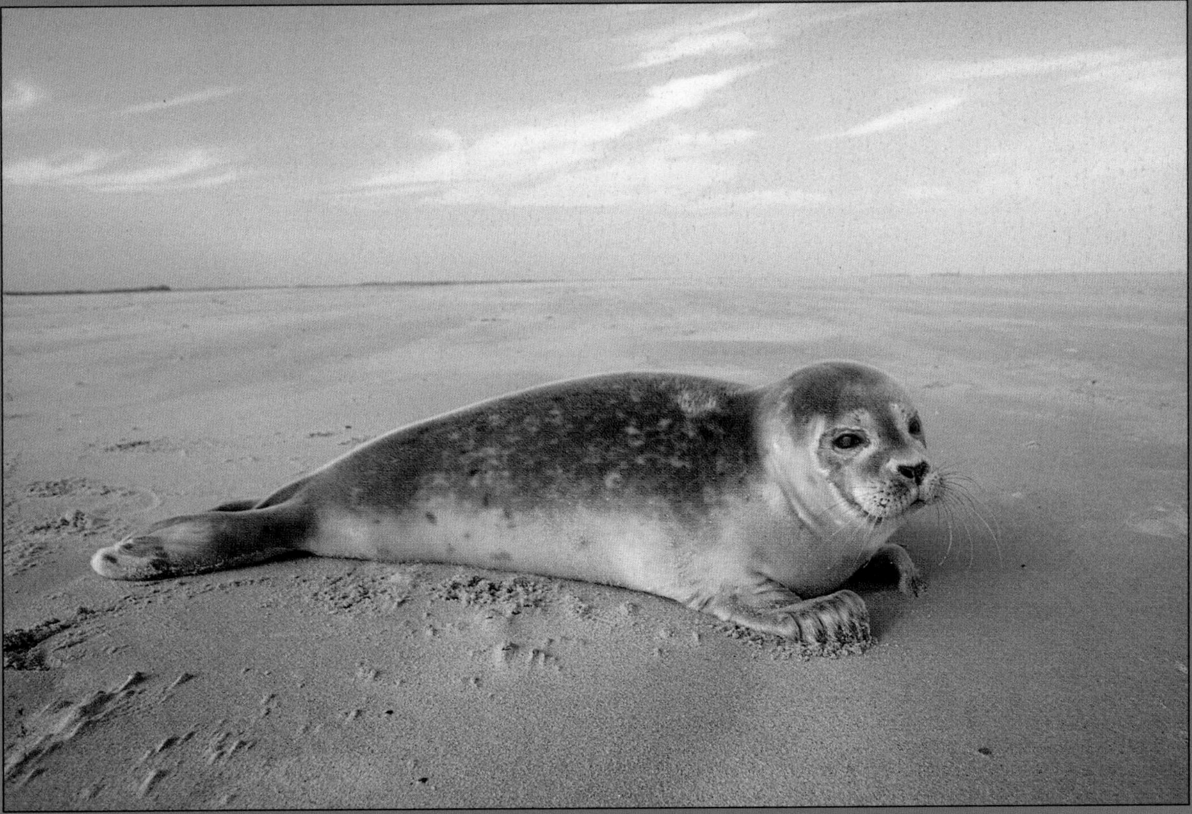

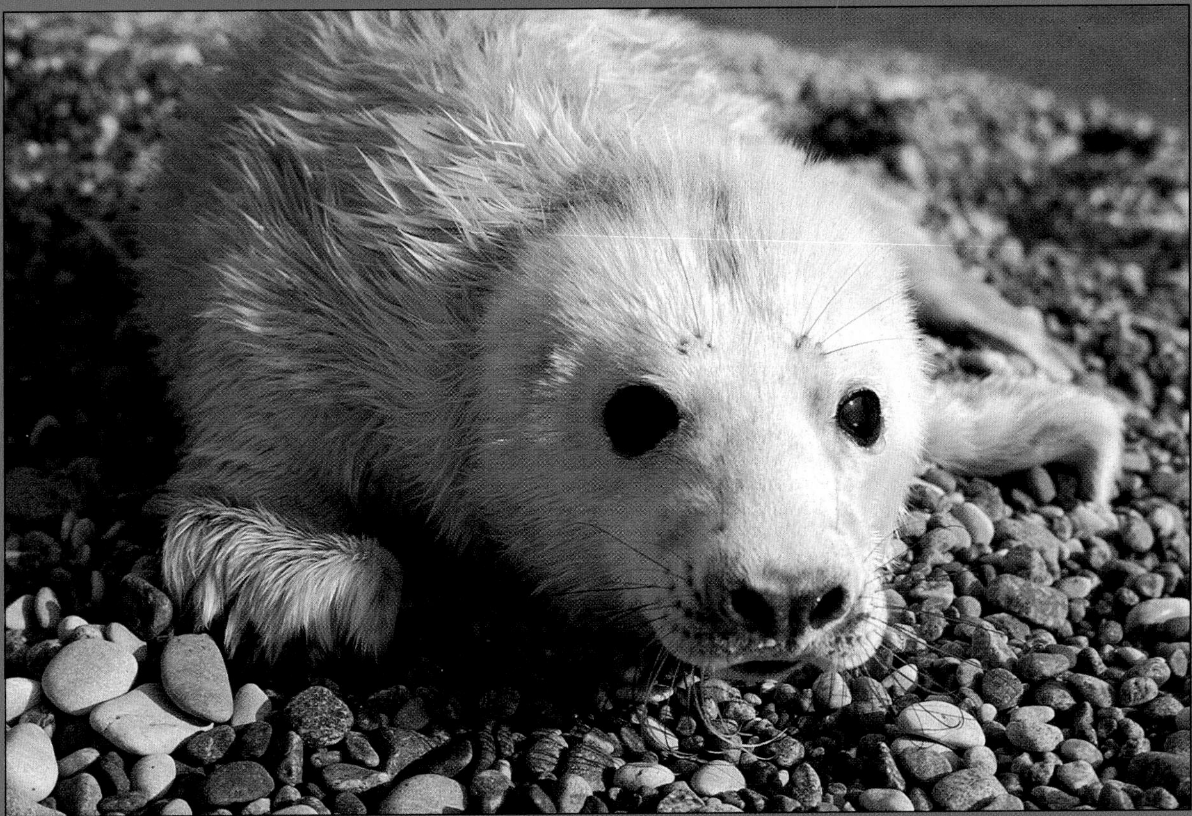

Seal Secret

William doesn't want to go "camping" with the local Welsh boy, Gwyn. He's very angry with his parents for bringing him on a cottage holiday in Wales. He'd rather be on their usual holiday — in a caravan right by the sea. But, Gwyn has a secret. He says that he will show it to William, as long as William swears not to tell anyone. They set off across the fields and down to the beach, where the secret is revealed.

Inside, the cave was not as deep as William expected. Really it was just a huge, spoon-shaped hole in the rock. But it echoed eerily the sound of the sea and the cries of gulls flying by outside.

The sandy floor was littered with boulders, rocks and pebbles. Gwyn picked a way through them. After a few yards he held out his arm, bringing William to a halt. Then he pointed to the back corner of the cave across from where they stood.

William squinted into the unusual light: gloomy, yet somehow bright too from sunlight reflected off the sea. At first he could pick out nothing but rocks.

Then one of the rocks moved.

"What is it?" he asked.

"Won't hurt," Gwyn said, "so long as you keep away from the business end."

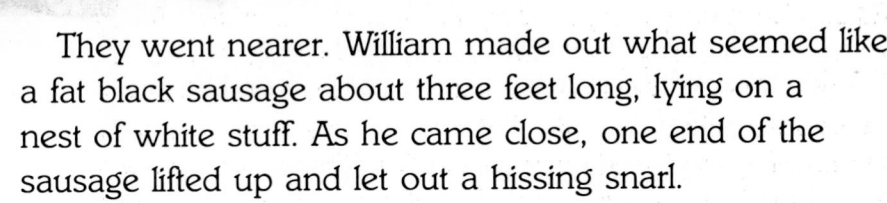

They went nearer. William made out what seemed like a fat black sausage about three feet long, lying on a nest of white stuff. As he came close, one end of the sausage lifted up and let out a hissing snarl.

"Seal pup," Gwyn said, stopping six feet away.

Now William could clearly see a soft dog-like head with fine whiskers fanning from its nose. No ears were visible but the eyes were large, chestnut brown, and sorrowful. Tears made a wet patch of fur under them as the pup stared up at him.

"It's crying!" he said, feeling he wanted to stroke the poor animal and comfort it.

"They always do," Gwyn said. "Dunno why. Daft, isn't it?"

"How did it get here?"

"Born here," Gwyn said. "I saw it happen." He could not disguise his pride.

"You saw it!" William said, envious. "Great! Was it . . ." He did not know how to say what he meant.

"About three weeks back," Gwyn said. "Just like our bitch having pups."

William did not dare tell Gwyn he had never seen a dog having pups. In fact, he had never seen any animal giving birth. Except in biology films at school, of course, and he knew that was not at all the same. "I wish I'd been here," he said.

"I couldn't get too close," Gwyn said. "They scare easy, see. Seals desert their young if they know there's people about."

William looked round anxiously. "Where's the mother now?"

"Gone."

"You mean we've scared her off?"

"No, she went last week. The pup is born, see, and the mother feeds it for about two weeks. After that she never comes back."

"What she do that for?" William said, indignant. "No wonder the poor thing is crying all the time."

Gwyn laughed. "Idiot. It's not crying because of that!"

"What then?"

"I dunno. But it's not that. They all do it. The mother did it as well."

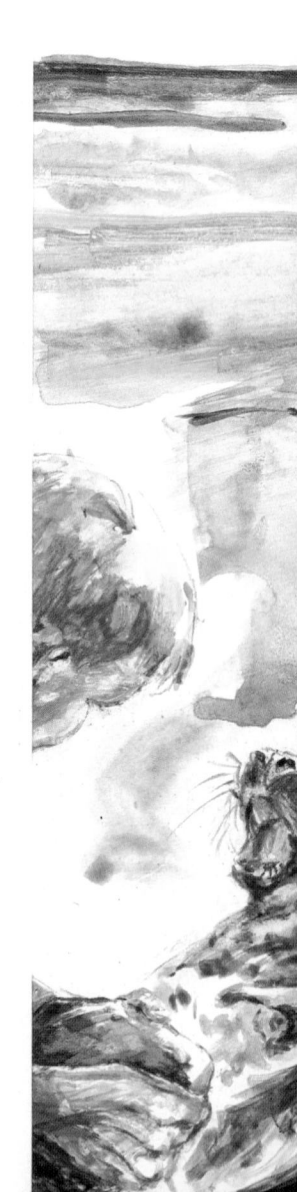

Gwyn started picking up large rocks and lugging them to within ten feet of the seal, where he set them down, one on another. William paid no attention, his eyes fixed on the pup. He found the animal fascinating, wanted to know all about it, wanted to touch it, wanted to watch everything it did.

"Why doesn't the mother take the pup with her, though?" The parent seal's heartlessness puzzled him.

Gwyn said, "A fisherman down Pentyn told me seals suckle their pups for two weeks then go back to sea. He says pups don't really like the sea. So they stay where the mother leaves them, living off their body fat. He says it's only hunger that drives them into the water in the end. They have to swim to get food. It's all instinct, you see."

"So this one has been all by itself for a week now and is slowly starving." William went a step nearer the pup and squatted on his haunches to take a closer look.

The velvet-covered bundle of fat shuffled on its front flipper-paws, raised its head and let out a noise that was half dog-snarl and half cat-hiss.

"They got a nasty bite," Gwyn said. He was still busy piling rocks in a row behind William.

"Their fur looks lovely," William said, admiring the sleek blackness.

"You can stroke it if you keep behind the head."

William edged forwards. The seal tried to swivel so that it could face him, but was either too heavy for its own strength or its flippers could not get enough grip on the sand.

His heart pounding at the excitement, William cautiously put out his hand and touched the pup's back.

To his surprise, the fur was not soft and fine as it looked, but coarse and stiff. It reminded him of the fur on a terrier dog.

At his touch, the pup tried harder than ever to twist and bite him. But its blubbery body, with thick rolls of flesh round the neck, prevented it from turning its head round far. All it could do was bleat and hiss and snarl while its eyes wept profuse tears.

William retreated a step or two. He hated causing the pup anxiety. "You're all right," he said soothingly. "There's nothing to be afraid of. I'm not going to hurt you." Without taking his eyes off the seal, he called to Gwyn, "What's that white stuff it's lying on?"

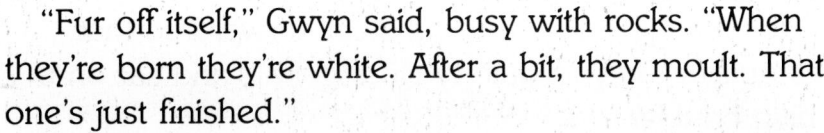

"Fur off itself," Gwyn said, busy with rocks. "When they're born they're white. After a bit, they moult. That one's just finished."

"Makes a nice bed."

"They're pretty when they're born. I expect that's why people like having coats made of their skins."

"That's cruel," William said. He had seen television news pictures of seal pups being killed. He had not liked watching.

"No different from killing lambs for meat, or cows come to that. You don't call that cruel, Billy-Will."

William turned to face Gwyn, ready to take up the argument. Instead his eyes caught sight of the rocks piled two feet high, starting at the cave wall and curving round the seal to meet the wall again.

"What's that for?" he asked.

"Ah!" Gwyn said, mysteriously. "Part of my plan, see."

"It's a wall."

"The boy's a genius!"

"But why?"

"To keep the seal in, bone-head."

William gaped at Gwyn, stunned.

"You're not going to try and keep it forever . . .?" he managed to say loudly enough for Gwyn to hear above the echoing sea and the cries of the pup.

Gwyn placed another rock, then came and stood by William.

"I'm going to teach it tricks, see. For a start anyway. For fun. But I've a better plan than that, Picasso."

William stared at Gwyn, unbelieving, hardly daring to ask the next question. He knew what the reply would be. The answer lay like a stone in his stomach, weighing him down, and crushing the excitement of seeing the seal.

He took a couple of stumbling steps forward so that he was outside Gwyn's quickly closing wall, and sat on a knee-high boulder.

Everything around him was all at once unpleasant. The air in the cave was cold, chilling. His clothes were cloying, sticky with damp salt water. His body felt weak and tired. Especially his legs. He looked at his legs, sculptured by his clinging jeans, to make sure they were not as match-stick thin as they felt. But they were.

"Want to know the rest of my plan?" Gwyn asked.

William could say nothing. His mouth might have been paralysed. He sat rigidly still.

Gwyn said, "I'm going to start a seal farm."

William let out a long sigh. His body slumped.

Gwyn stood looking across the wall at the seal, like a farmer admiring a new addition to his herd.

"With the shortage of food in the world," he went on, "I reckon seals would be a good bet. My Da is always going on about food and how there's too many people. He says that's why farming is a good job. Plenty of future in it, see. So I thought, nobody farms seals, and we've plenty round here. We could make special pens on the beach. There'd be meat, you see, and skins for fur coats as well. Good profit. Can't go wrong, man. And I could be first."

Gwyn was so excited, talking so fast, it was hard to sort out the words because of his accent.

William forced himself to look at Gwyn. "But you c-c-can't!" he said.

"Why not? We farm cows and sheep and hens and pigs and all sorts. There's even people farm fish, my Da says. So why not seals?"

"I don't know," William said desperately. "It just wouldn't be . . . right . . ."

"What's wrong with it? You tell me, genius." There was angry spite in Gwyn's voice now. He never liked being opposed.

"That seal," William said, trying hard to sort out what he really did think, and to stay calm in the face of Gwyn's rage, "that seal . . . it's wild. It's not like a pet . . . not like a dog . . . and it's not like a farm animal. It shouldn't be penned in. It's wild . . ."

"Rubbish!" Gwyn exploded. His face flushed bright red. His body stiffened. "Everything was wild once. You have to start somewhere."

William pushed himself to his feet and went to the wall. The pup turned its sorrowful eyes on him.

"But it's cruel," William said, almost pleading now. "You wouldn't be able to look after it properly. You d-d-don't know how."

"I can find out can't I? If it doesn't work I can always let the pup go," Gwyn said. "Anyway, what do you know about it? You're a city kid. A soft city kid. You don't know nothing about animals."

At that moment something inside William snapped. His desperation turned to anger. He rounded on Gwyn and shouted, "It'll be too late then." His voice echoed among the sea-birds' cries. "It'll be too weak to look after itself. Or it won't know how to swim and it'll be too late to learn."

He was looking for any argument that might help. But Gwyn's burning face and fierce eyes showed he was only getting more and more annoyed.

"It could die," William blurted out finally.

"It won't!" Gwyn yelled back. "I won't let it." He scuttled away, picked up another rock, scampered back, piled it on to the wall. "I don't care what you say, English. That seal is mine. I'm keeping it. And I'll do what I want with it."

William shook with anger. With fear too. Fear at what he must say and do. He took a deep breath, gathering himself together.

"No." He spoke firmly and without stammering, despite his churning insides. "No, you won't."

Slowly Gwyn came from the wall, fists clenched, and stood squared up close to William. "Oh?" he said with cool menace. "And who's going to stop me?"

William braced himself.

"I am," he heard himself say, as though someone else were speaking the words.

Gwyn glowered. "You!" he said. "You couldn't knock the skin off a rice pudding."

"Think what you like," William said, "but I'm not letting you keep that seal."

Gwyn's fist smashed into William's nose.

The force of the blow sent him staggering back. His feet hit a rock, he tripped, and went sprawling to the ground.

Before he could pick himself up, stones were hitting him hard on the body.

Gwyn was shouting, "You get out of here, English rubbish! You hear? Scat! Leave my seal alone!"

Stumbling, dabbing at his bleeding nose, scrambling through the litter of rocks, William fled out of the cave, stones hailing after him.

He was in the sea up to his knees before he was out of Gwyn's range. He stopped and turned. He could hardly see for tears of pain swamping his eyes. Whenever he sniffed, he tasted the iron flavour of blood.

Gwyn was standing at the entrance of the cave like a guard before a fortress gate. "And don't forget," he shouted, anger still strident in his voice. "You swore, boy. You took an oath. You tell and I'll sort you out, see."

There was nothing to be done. William plodded slowly away towards the beach. The tide had gone farther; the walk to shore was easier than the walk to the cave.

But he hardly noticed anyway. His mind tumbled with anger and humiliation.

"He's a fool!" William said aloud. "An idiot! His brains are pickled."

He bent as he waded to splash water on to his face. Salt stung in his wounded nose. A trace of blood swirled away on the tide.

When he reached the shore, he looked back at the cave. Gwyn was still standing there, watching, a small, almost invisible figure from this distance.

'I'm going to get that seal out of there, Gwyn Davies," William shouted. He picked up a pebble and hurled it with all his force into the sea. "I'm going to rescue that seal, I don't care what you do to stop me."

Aidan Chambers
Illustrated by Pat Serninger   **49**

It's my home

WALES

Road signs in bot English and Welsh can be found on the borders between England and Wales. We learn to speak an write Welsh in school.

As king of England during the thirteenth century, I spent many years trying to conquer Wales. To do this, I built castles around the country. A number are still there today.

● = Castles in Wales

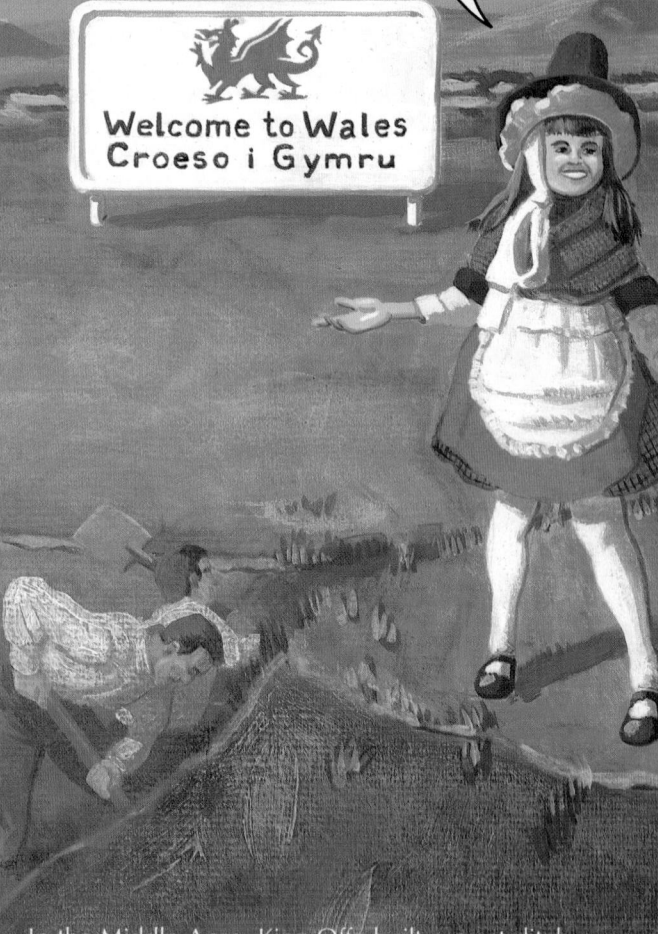

Welcome to Wales
Croeso i Gymru

In the Middle Ages, King Offa built a great ditch and bank stretching from north to south Wales. This was called Offa's Dyke and was a barrier between the fighting English and Welsh tribes. Today Offa's Dyke Path marks this old border between England and Wales.

There are many mountains in Wales. The most famous peak is Snowdon – 1,085 metres high – which stands within the Snowdonia National Park. You can walk to the top of Mount Snowdon by following any one of six marked paths. Alternatively, you can let the mountain train take the strain!

The National Eisteddfod, held each year at the beginning of August, is a celebration of the best in Welsh music, poetry and drama. The ceremony of the Chairing of the Bard names the person chosen as one of the best Welsh poets for that year.

Mining is important in Wales. You can spot a coalmine by the tower and the wheel which works the lift going underground.

Rugby is the national game of Wales. Home international games are played at Cardiff Arms Park stadium.

Meet the PRINCE of

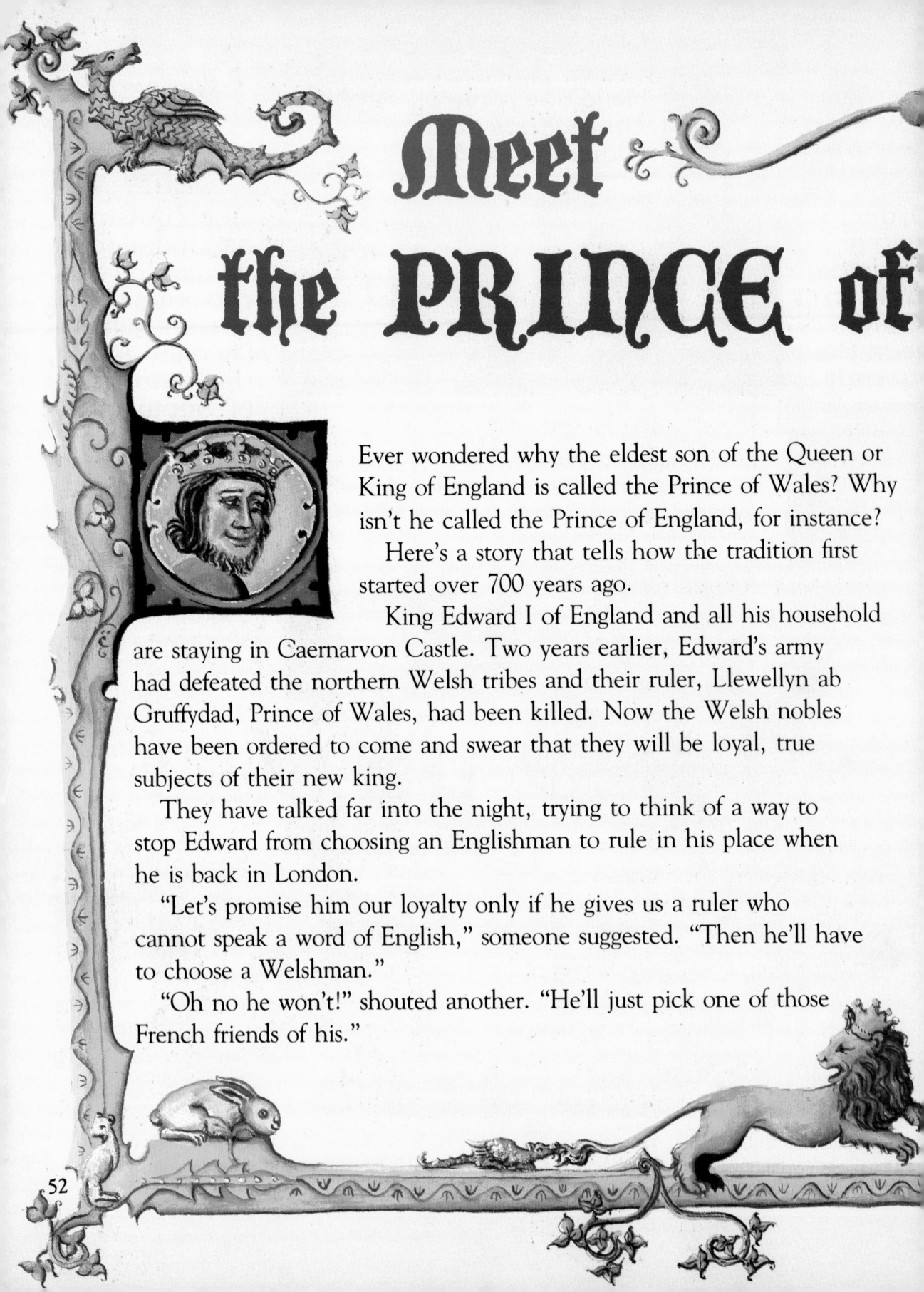

Ever wondered why the eldest son of the Queen or King of England is called the Prince of Wales? Why isn't he called the Prince of England, for instance?

Here's a story that tells how the tradition first started over 700 years ago.

King Edward I of England and all his household are staying in Caernarvon Castle. Two years earlier, Edward's army had defeated the northern Welsh tribes and their ruler, Llewellyn ab Gruffydad, Prince of Wales, had been killed. Now the Welsh nobles have been ordered to come and swear that they will be loyal, true subjects of their new king.

They have talked far into the night, trying to think of a way to stop Edward from choosing an Englishman to rule in his place when he is back in London.

"Let's promise him our loyalty only if he gives us a ruler who cannot speak a word of English," someone suggested. "Then he'll have to choose a Welshman."

"Oh no he won't!" shouted another. "He'll just pick one of those French friends of his."

WALES

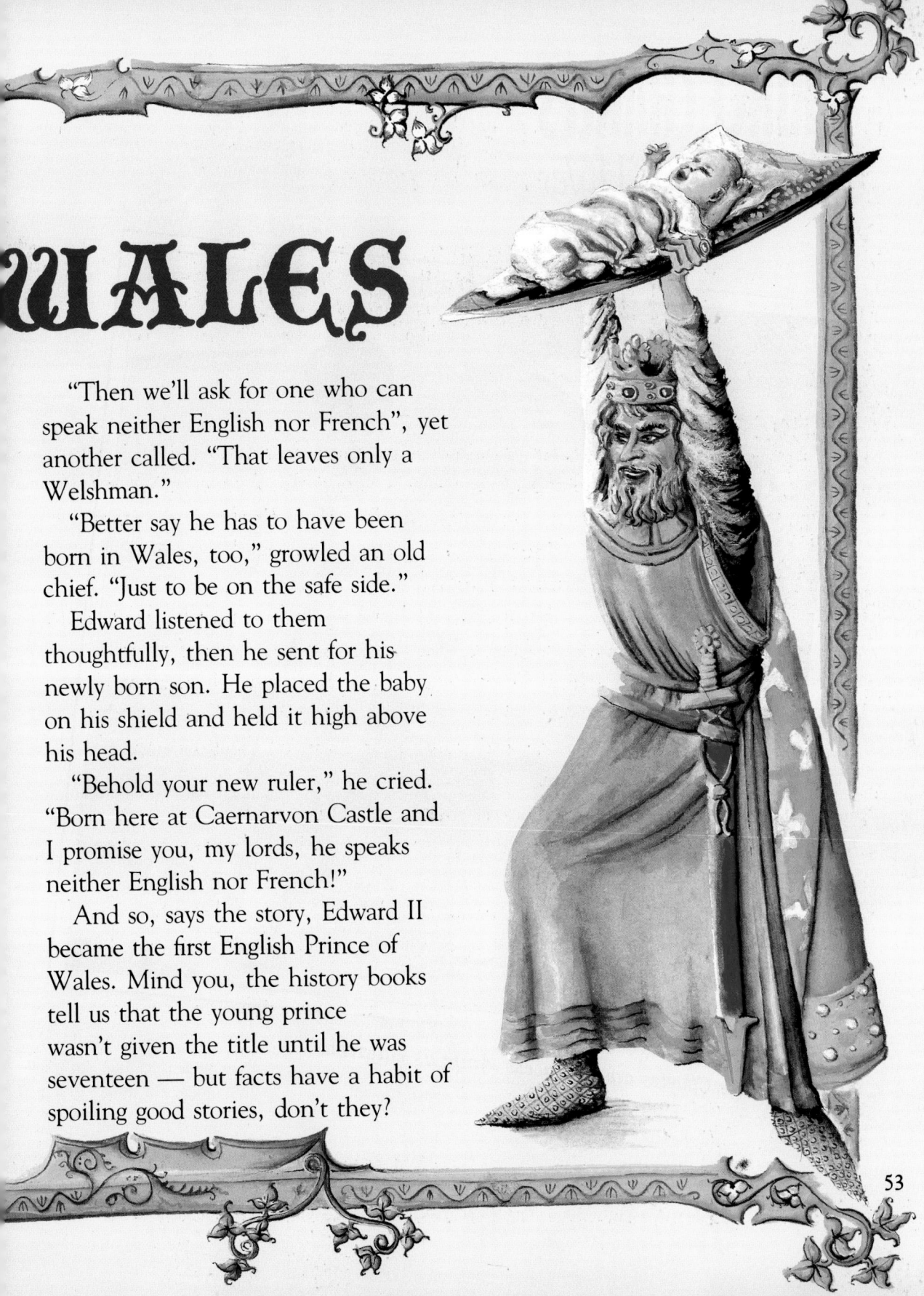

"Then we'll ask for one who can speak neither English nor French", yet another called. "That leaves only a Welshman."

"Better say he has to have been born in Wales, too," growled an old chief. "Just to be on the safe side."

Edward listened to them thoughtfully, then he sent for his newly born son. He placed the baby on his shield and held it high above his head.

"Behold your new ruler," he cried. "Born here at Caernarvon Castle and I promise you, my lords, he speaks neither English nor French!"

And so, says the story, Edward II became the first English Prince of Wales. Mind you, the history books tell us that the young prince wasn't given the title until he was seventeen — but facts have a habit of spoiling good stories, don't they?

PRINCE CHARLES
Prince of Wales

Prince Charles and Princess Anne as children.

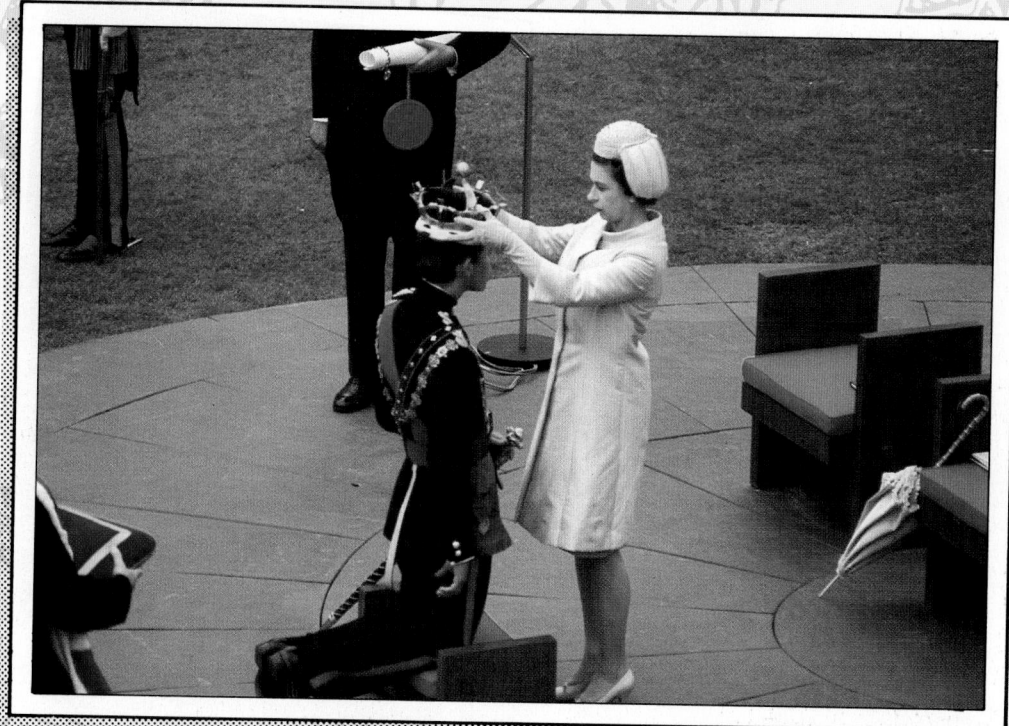

In 1969 Charles was made Prince of Wales
by the Queen at Caernarvon Castle.

The Prince and Princess of Wales on their wedding day.

PRINCE CHARLES
Prince of Wales

Prince Charles enjoys playing polo.

Prince Charles is greeted by a child while visiting Liverpool.

Charles talks to workers on a visit to a factory in Birmingham.

Charles enjoys painting very much. Here he is painting in Japan.

Dear Godmother

15 Sevensecrets Street
Little Upsley

25th November

Dear Godmother,

I'm sorry I haven't written since the holidays, but things have been pretty hectic around here lately. (In fact, frantic would be a better word.) Some of it has been exciting and some of it funny, but some bits are a bit worrying.

You remember how when I was staying with you and you told me you had all those magic powers and made me promise I would keep your secret for ever and a day? Well, I wonder if we could shorten that time span a little?

The main problem has been all those presents you gave me. Please don't think that I wasn't impressed. I mean, who wouldn't want a pair of seven-league trainers? The only thing is, I didn't know until I tried them on that a league is about 4.5 km. (Maybe you'd forgotten that, too?) Anyway, I kept them till the school sports and didn't put them on till I was at the starting line. I took one step and WHAM! – I was way out in the country! It took me a while to work out what had happened and then when I tried to step back to the sports field something went wrong and I landed in the middle of the village duck pond. I got some nasty looks from passers-by and one old man wanted to call a policeman but I pretended I'd lost my memory. Then I sneaked off while they were all arguing about whether I had something they called amkneesyer (well, that's how it sounded).

I had to take my trainers off and walk back to school in my bare feet, wet clothes and all, and by the time I got there all the races I was going to run in were over, even the three-legged one. (Jo still isn't talking to me and that was three weeks ago.) Then I got into awful trouble from the teacher for going swimming without permission (and in my sports gear too). And for the next week I had the worst cold I've ever had in my life. Please don't think I don't like the trainers. It's just that they're a bit difficult to control. I've put them in a box in the back of the wardrobe in case I get kidnapped or mixed up in a hold-up or something. I mean they might come in handy, providing the robber or kidnapper gives me time to go home and change my shoes.

I was really excited about the jumper of invisibility. But making it the same colour as my school one wasn't such a good idea after all. It worked fine for disappearing when the teacher wanted someone to pick up litter in the playground and when the Head was checking on who was late for class. (You were right about people not really noticing, providing you don't disappear when they're looking straight at you — they just think you've sloped off without saying anything.) Where it went wrong was on the week of the school camp. Mum insisted that I had to take the jumper you'd so kindly given me and stuffed my old one in the dustbin to stop me swapping behind her back. But camp is such fun I didn't want to miss ANYTHING! The trouble was, it was freezing cold and everyone kept telling me I was crazy to be going round in just a T-shirt and I kept pretending that I was feeling fine. (It was really hard because my teeth kept chattering and kids kept saying my face was all blue.) By the time we got on the bus to come home I was running a temperature. (Mrs Davies kept saying, "I told you you'd get sick. You make sure your mother knows it's your own fault!") Anyway, I got the worst dose of 'flu I've ever had and I've had to hide the jumper with my trainers and pretend I've lost it and Mum is absolutely FURIOUS and is threatening to write a letter to the Head about how careless the teachers are and about lost property.

But why I want you to let me tell about your secret is because the never-empty purse has got me into real trouble. It was terrific fun taking out the gold coin and immediately finding another one in its place. I did that quite a lot until I had a whole heap of them. But then I got bored, so I hid them in my underwear drawer. I didn't like to leave the purse at home so I took it to school with me. On the way I found I'd forgotten my dinner money, so I went into the shop to ask Mrs Wilkins if she could cash a gold coin. (Yes, I know it was stupid of me.) Anyway, she told my teacher and my teacher took me to the Head and they both wanted to know where I'd got such a rare and valuable coin from and did my parents know I had it. I said I'd found it (which was kind of true) and they wanted to know where, so I said "in the street" (which wasn't true but what could I say?) Well, of course, they didn't believe me and then the Head rang home and it turned out Mum had found the coins in my drawer when she was putting away my clean pants and she was upset and I was sent home in disgrace.

So, here I am, shut up in my room waiting for Dad to come home, and I know he'll be mad at me too, because as Mum said, it's possible to find one gold coin in the street but not 389 of them. I've been trying to think of a better story but I can't. I'm really worried because if Mum and Dad go to the police to try to find the owner, as Mum says they'll do, then the police might decide to keep me in jail while they investigate and I don't think the Head would ever forgive me if I became a criminal.(He's always going on about the good name of the school.)

I do wish you had a telephone as it's going to be awful waiting for a reply from you. As it is I'm going to have to put on my jumper of invisibility so I can sneak out and post this.(It _is_ handy, I must admit!) Luckily there's a letter box only two doors down so I should get away with it. But please answer straight away. Either that or wave a wand or something and give Mum and Dad and the Head amkneesyer so they forget all about it.

Your loving, but distressed god-daughter,

Samantha.

P.S. Perhaps you could send a pair of seven-league shoes for my teacher for when she wants to get away from us all (I think she'd take size 7) and a jumper of invisibility for the Head so he can sneak around better (he's short and fat) and a purse of their own for Mum and Dad so they can buy the new car they want. Then they'd all have to keep quiet.

P.P.S. You haven't got a turn-back-time-clock by any chance, have you?

Pat Edwards

SECRET RIDDLES

Strange Journey or Strange Dream?

It is Monday morning and Jennifer is on the school bus on her way to school. She should have written a composition, called "My Strangest Dream", over the weekend, but she hadn't been able to think of any dreams. Closing her eyes, she tries to let her thoughts wander. With a sudden jolt, Jennifer opens her eyes to find that she is no longer in the bus, but riding alone in a big, beautiful carriage. At first she thinks it is a trick or a joke arranged by her friends, or that maybe she has gone mad. Then she remembers what she had been thinking about. Yes, she must be having a dream! In the carriage she notices a drawer. Jennifer opens it to find some unusual clothes.

Ordinarily Jennifer was not the sort of person who greatly cared for frocks and silver slippers, or even pearl necklaces. But this was a kind of special occasion, she felt, and besides, there was nothing else to do. So, after looking around once again just to make sure that no one was watching, she took off her jeans and her shirt, folded them carefully into the drawer and slipped on the yellow dress.

Strangely enough it fitted her perfectly; it seemed almost to have been made for her. Next she tried on the stockings and the shoes. The shoes were rather uncomfortable, being silver, but they weren't as heavy as she had expected. Then she fastened the pearls around

her neck, put on the sky-blue cloak with the jewelled clasp and shut the drawer with her own clothes in it, feeling very naughty and rather grand at the same time.

Hardly had she sat down again, though, than she realised with a start that the carriage had slowed down. Turning to the window, she looked out and found herself on a street in a great city. It was filled with people dressed in strange costumes, and lined with quaint-looking shops and little stalls selling, besides food and other commonplace things, many strange articles that Jennifer could not identify.

A stream of carriages was passing by in the other direction, though none was as large or luxurious as the one in which she was riding. To Jennifer's astonishment, everyone who caught sight of her peering out from behind the lace curtains (and they all seemed to be looking her way) would stand very respectfully facing her and bow low as she passed by.

It's these clothes, she thought in sudden panic. They're mistaking me for someone else. What will they do when they find out? I'd better change back right now!

But at that very moment the carriage turned through an ornate gate onto a broad avenue. Ahead Jennifer could see a huge palace with high towers and spires, fountains on the lawn in front.

A guard of resplendently uniformed soldiers lined up on the steps leading to the doors. There the carriage stopped. It was too late to get back into her old clothes now.

The carriage door swung open and a tall man with dark, stern eyes strode towards her with his hand outstretched.

"I-I-I'm sorry about the clothes!" Jennifer stammered, her face scarlet. "Really I am! I know I shouldn't be wearing them."

But the man appeared not to hear her.

"Welcome!" he said in a voice that seemed to come from the soles of his red leather boots. He bowed solemnly even as he helped her down onto the grass. "It is pleasant to see your Highness looking so well."

Your Highness! This dream was certainly becoming more interesting! What did this man take her for, a queen or something? Jennifer tried to put on her most ladylike manner.

"Thank you very much," she replied. "And who may you be, sir?" She almost added, "And who may *I* be, for that matter?" but thought better of it.

"I am Duke Rinaldo, your Highness," the man told her gravely. "Lord High Chancellor of your Highness's most loyal realm of Eladeria. Amongst other duties."

"Congratulations," said Jennifer, although it didn't seem quite the correct reply. Then she said, "Where is the driver of my carriage, if you please? I would like to see that he or she is rewarded for my very comfortable journey."

Actually she only wanted to see the driver's face, just to satisfy her earlier curiosity, but the idea of royally rewarding someone was pleasing too.

"Driver, your Highness?" inquired Rinaldo, a ghost of a smile playing on his thin lips. "Did your Highness not know? There *was* no driver." He held up a long, bony finger, pointing behind her. "And see —"

Following his gesture, Jennifer turned around and gasped. There was no sign of carriage or horses to be seen.

"But how — That is, I should have heard —"

She looked about her at the faces of the many splendid attendants standing nearby. None of them seemed aware that anything out of the ordinary had taken place.

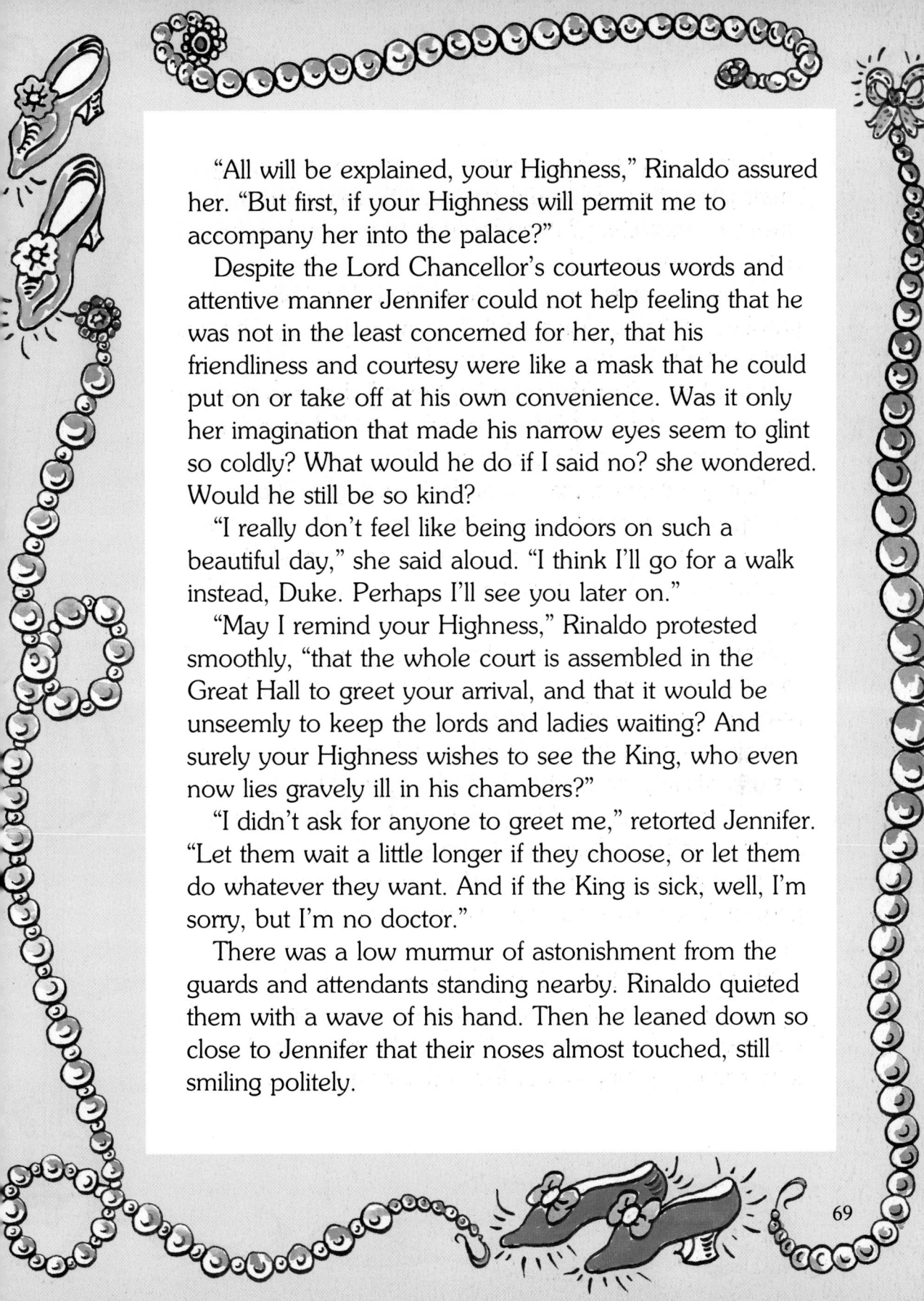

"All will be explained, your Highness," Rinaldo assured her. "But first, if your Highness will permit me to accompany her into the palace?"

Despite the Lord Chancellor's courteous words and attentive manner Jennifer could not help feeling that he was not in the least concerned for her, that his friendliness and courtesy were like a mask that he could put on or take off at his own convenience. Was it only her imagination that made his narrow eyes seem to glint so coldly? What would he do if I said no? she wondered. Would he still be so kind?

"I really don't feel like being indoors on such a beautiful day," she said aloud. "I think I'll go for a walk instead, Duke. Perhaps I'll see you later on."

"May I remind your Highness," Rinaldo protested smoothly, "that the whole court is assembled in the Great Hall to greet your arrival, and that it would be unseemly to keep the lords and ladies waiting? And surely your Highness wishes to see the King, who even now lies gravely ill in his chambers?"

"I didn't ask for anyone to greet me," retorted Jennifer. "Let them wait a little longer if they choose, or let them do whatever they want. And if the King is sick, well, I'm sorry, but I'm no doctor."

There was a low murmur of astonishment from the guards and attendants standing nearby. Rinaldo quieted them with a wave of his hand. Then he leaned down so close to Jennifer that their noses almost touched, still smiling politely.

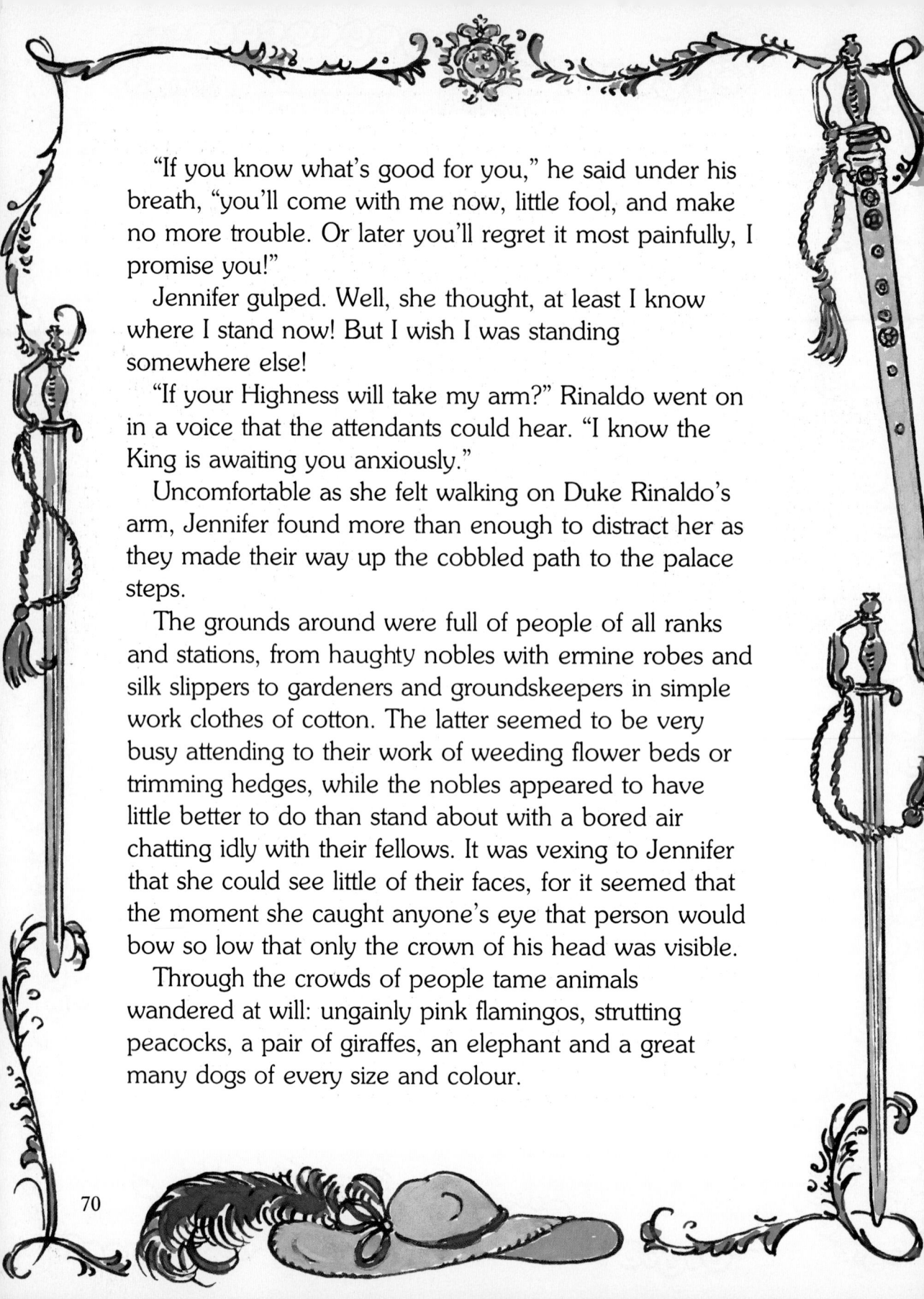

"If you know what's good for you," he said under his breath, "you'll come with me now, little fool, and make no more trouble. Or later you'll regret it most painfully, I promise you!"

Jennifer gulped. Well, she thought, at least I know where I stand now! But I wish I was standing somewhere else!

"If your Highness will take my arm?" Rinaldo went on in a voice that the attendants could hear. "I know the King is awaiting you anxiously."

Uncomfortable as she felt walking on Duke Rinaldo's arm, Jennifer found more than enough to distract her as they made their way up the cobbled path to the palace steps.

The grounds around were full of people of all ranks and stations, from haughty nobles with ermine robes and silk slippers to gardeners and groundskeepers in simple work clothes of cotton. The latter seemed to be very busy attending to their work of weeding flower beds or trimming hedges, while the nobles appeared to have little better to do than stand about with a bored air chatting idly with their fellows. It was vexing to Jennifer that she could see little of their faces, for it seemed that the moment she caught anyone's eye that person would bow so low that only the crown of his head was visible.

Through the crowds of people tame animals wandered at will: ungainly pink flamingos, strutting peacocks, a pair of giraffes, an elephant and a great many dogs of every size and colour.

On the palace steps, which were built of marble and stood out from the huge building itself in a wide half-circle, a triple row of guards stood stiffly to attention at either side. Their armour was polished till it hurt the eyes; their long straight swords hung from their hips in ruby-studded scabbards. The moment Jennifer set her foot on each step of the broad stairway, the guards on that step would lift their swords high into the air and cry "Hail!" in such deafening voices that her head was aching long before she reached the top.

At last, though, they came to the great double doors. At a sign from Duke Rinaldo these were flung open with a flourish of trumpets from heralds standing nearby. The procession moved inside with Jennifer at the front, trying to look more royal than she felt.

She found herself in the Great Hall. The huge room had a floor of inlaid marble and a domed roof that seemed impossibly high. The tapestried walls were lined with page-boys, ladies-in-waiting and innumerable other courtiers, all bowing and curtseying towards her at once.

Before Jennifer had had time to take this in properly, however, there was a commotion from one side and in burst a figure like none she had ever seen. It was a dwarf, no taller than Jennifer herself, dressed in the pied costume of a court jester with cap, bells and huge pointed slippers turned up at the toes. This strange creature tumbled into the hall in such a flurry of cartwheels and pratfalls that Jennifer could not help but laugh, especially when he somersaulted through mid-air to land at her very feet, all but knocking her down.

"Insolent dog!" Rinaldo growled. "You shall be whipped for this! Yes, and you shall sleep in the stables for a week!"

"He shall do no such thing!" exclaimed Jennifer, deciding that she had better take charge of this dream before it got completely out of hand. "No, he should be rewarded rather!"

She turned to the small figure of the jester with interest. The dwarf had fallen back a few paces and was regarding her keenly with his bright eyes.

"What is your name, sir?" Jennifer inquired politely. "What shall I call you?"

At the word "sir" Rinaldo cringed, but the dwarf ignored him.

"Why, Highness," he replied in a sing-song voice, "my name is Samson. But as for what you shall call me, that is up to you. Insolent Dog is popular this season. Also Peabrain, Crookface, Worm, Stinkweed and Monkey." He nodded at Rinaldo. "My Lord the Chancellor could doubtless suggest more names, Highness, if those do not please you."

Rinaldo glowered and roughly drew Samson aside by the shoulder.

"When I have done with you, fool of a Fool," he hissed softly, "your names shall be Gap-Tooth, One-Eye and Peg-Leg. I know your mind, lack-witted jester. You seek to use the Princess against me, hoping at the same time that she will protect you. Simpleton! What do I care for any feeble scheme of yours? And who will protect you when she is gone?"

"Why do you whisper, my Lord?" returned the jester in a voice loud enough for Jennifer to hear. "In the presence of her Highness you should display better manners! And do not seek to bully me as you bully others. For all the beatings I have suffered at your command, Rinaldo, for all the days without food and the sleepless nights in the stables, yes, and for all your insults and mockery you shall yet pay!"

Jennifer scowled. So that was how Rinaldo enforced his authority! With threats, with beatings, with starvation

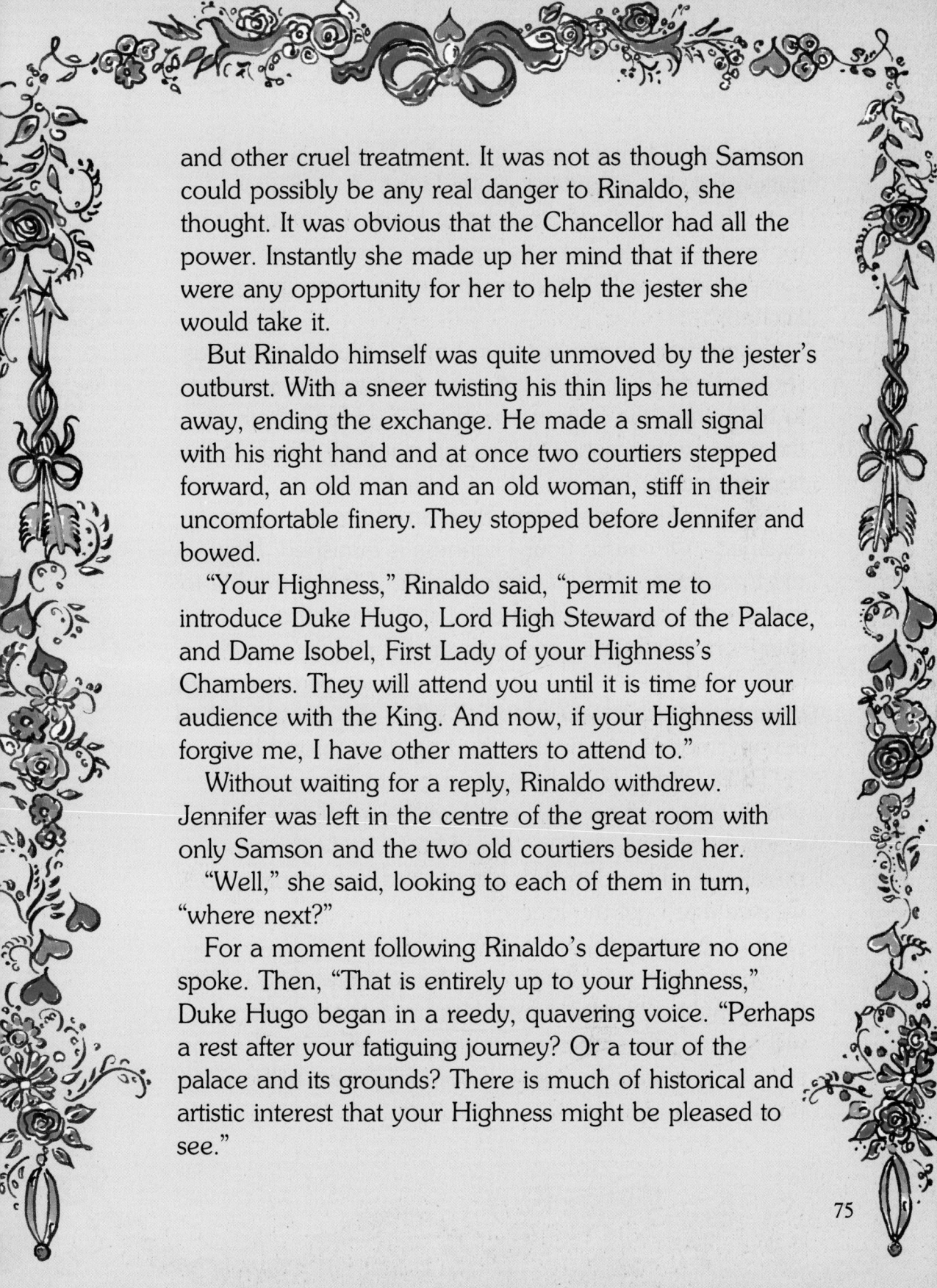

and other cruel treatment. It was not as though Samson could possibly be any real danger to Rinaldo, she thought. It was obvious that the Chancellor had all the power. Instantly she made up her mind that if there were any opportunity for her to help the jester she would take it.

But Rinaldo himself was quite unmoved by the jester's outburst. With a sneer twisting his thin lips he turned away, ending the exchange. He made a small signal with his right hand and at once two courtiers stepped forward, an old man and an old woman, stiff in their uncomfortable finery. They stopped before Jennifer and bowed.

"Your Highness," Rinaldo said, "permit me to introduce Duke Hugo, Lord High Steward of the Palace, and Dame Isobel, First Lady of your Highness's Chambers. They will attend you until it is time for your audience with the King. And now, if your Highness will forgive me, I have other matters to attend to."

Without waiting for a reply, Rinaldo withdrew. Jennifer was left in the centre of the great room with only Samson and the two old courtiers beside her.

"Well," she said, looking to each of them in turn, "where next?"

For a moment following Rinaldo's departure no one spoke. Then, "That is entirely up to your Highness," Duke Hugo began in a reedy, quavering voice. "Perhaps a rest after your fatiguing journey? Or a tour of the palace and its grounds? There is much of historical and artistic interest that your Highness might be pleased to see."

"No," said Jennifer apologetically, "I don't think I'm quite ready for a tour yet, Duke Hugo. As a matter of fact, what I'd really like is a bit of lunch if it wouldn't be too much trouble. I can fix myself a sandwich or something if you'll just show me where I can find the kitchen."

"Your Highness fix her own lunch?" Hugo's tone was shocked and Dame Isobel turned deathly pale and had to hold on to the Duke for support. Suddenly both of them threw themselves down and put their heads to the floor at Jennifer's feet.

"Alas, I am nothing more than an old fool!" Hugo moaned. "Of course your Highness is famished. How did I not think of it? It is unforgivable! Do not trouble to call the guards, your Highness. I shall go to the dungeons this minute and lock myself in!"

And with these words the pitiful old steward arose and would really have taken himself off to the dungeons had Jennifer not caught him by the arm to comfort him.

"There, there, Hugo!" she said gently. "I'm sure you've had a lot on your mind with a royal visit to get ready for and all. Anyone could have made the same mistake. And besides, if you go to the dungeons, who will see that I get my lunch?"

Hugo brightened somewhat at this.

"That is true, your Highness," he said gratefully. "I had not thought of that. If it please your Highness, then, I will have a little something sent up to your chambers as soon as it can be arranged. If your Highness will excuse me?"

Jennifer nodded and Hugo went off as rapidly as his stiff clothes and his dignity would permit.

"Good," Jennifer said to Dame Isobel, who was still in shock at the thought of royalty preparing its own lunch, and to Samson, who had watched the whole scene with a twinkle of wry amusement in his eyes. "Now that that's settled, will you guide me to my chamber please, Dame Isobel? And you, Samson, do come with us."

They travelled up a long corridor lined with dark and musty portraits ("Your ancestors!" Samson told Jennifer with a strange laugh) which led to another chamber, not so large or bright as the first, with arched passageways opening from it in many directions.

Down one of these Dame Isobel guided them, past doorways on the left and on the right, and across more passages, till suddenly they came to a small door which opened onto a sunny and spacious courtyard.

In it was a pool fed by a fountain in the shape of a miniature spouting whale. Fawns gambolled on the grass nearby, coming at times to drink at the edge of the pool. From a window high overhead came the music of lute and recorder playing a stately air with a long-ago sound to it. It was so sweet that Jennifer longed to be able to stay and hear more.

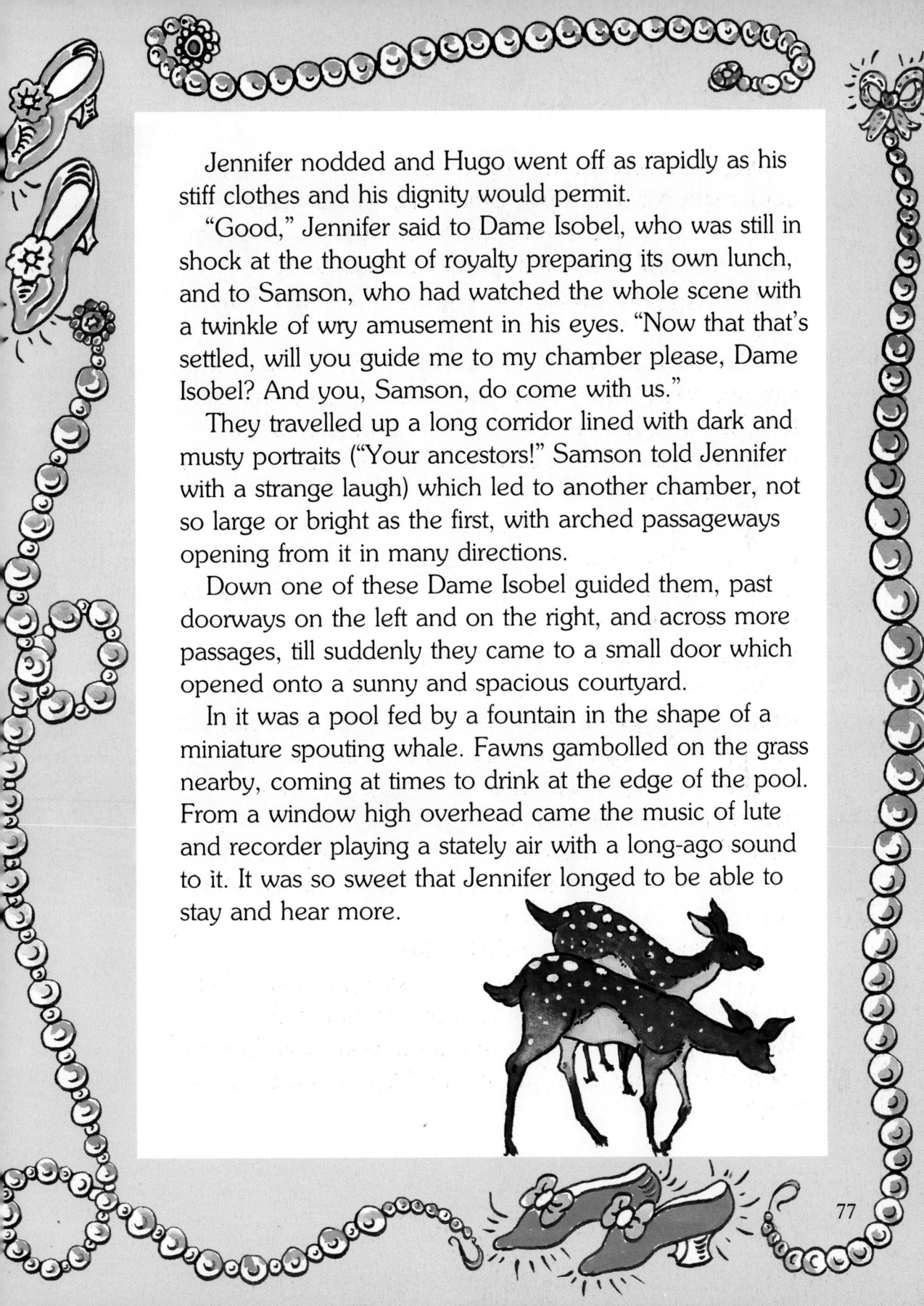

"Such a dream!" she sighed. "It would be a pity to wake up now!"

Nick Sullivan
Illustrated by Sandra Laroche

Magicians always say it, don't they?
What does it mean?

Abracadabra was probably the name of an ancient demon, imagined by people long ago. In those times it was believed that once you knew the name of the supernatural being, you could use it as a charm. Just calling out Abracadabra's name would work magic, they thought.

Doctors in early Roman times tried it as a cure for diseases like flu and toothache, and in time it became a secret, magic word. It was written in this special way on parchment and hung round the patient's neck on a linen thread.

```
A B R A C A D A B R A
A B R A C A D A B R
A B R A C A D A B
A B R A C A D A
A B R A C A D
A B R A C A
A B R A C
A B R A
A B R
A B
A
```

Did it work?
What do you think?

Special days

Saint David's Day

1 MARCH

Who was Saint David?

Saint David, or Dewi Sant as the Welsh call him, lived sometime in the sixth century. All that is definitely known about him is that he was a Christian missionary who became the Bishop of Menevia in southern Wales. He was made a saint in AD 1120 by Pope Calixtus II.

Why is he remembered?

There are many stories and legends about Saint David. Some of these say that he was the uncle of King Arthur — even though many English tales claim that Arthur was born in Cornwall. Others describe his skill as a preacher and declare that miraculous things happened while he was speaking. At one meeting, so the story goes, a white dove flew down and perched on David's shoulder. At the same time the ground beneath his feet rose, lifting him high above the crowd so all could see and hear him clearly.

Many legends link the saint with the leek plant. It was said that when David died, his people wept bitterly. Wherever their tears fell to earth, leek plants sprang to life. The favourite legend, however, is the one which tells of the battle between the Welsh and the Saxons who were trying to invade Wales. The Welsh were losing.

"I know why!" cried a Welsh monk. "The enemy soldiers are wearing the same kind of clothes as our own soldiers. It's hard to tell friend from foe."

He bent down and pulled a leek from the ground.

"Let each Welshman wear a leek in his helmet," he shouted, "then you will know who not to strike down."

The Welsh soldiers did as he said, charged the enemy again — and won! The monk was David, says the legend, and it is in his honour that many Welsh people wear a leek on St David's Day.

Schools in Wales often hold an eisteddfod (a celebration of songs, sketches and plays) on St David's Day. Children dress up in traditional costume to take part and watch.

Forgetful Fred.

No point in sharing a secret with Fred. He's so absent-minded he'd promptly forget it — or forget to keep it a secret and tell the first person he met.

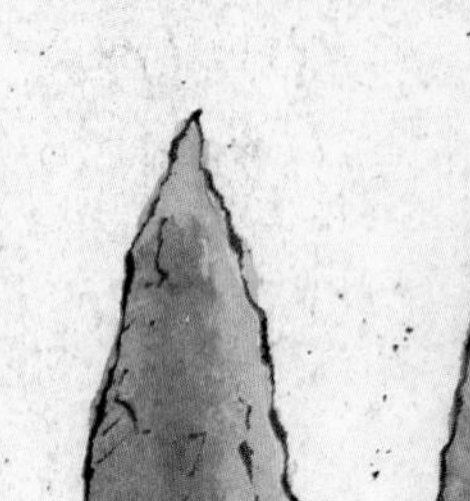

The richest man in the land, even richer than the king, was Bumberdumble Pott. He lived in an enormous house with forty-four rooms, and he had nine cooks, twelve housemaids, four butlers, sixteen helpers, and a young man named Fred who did everything that was left over.

Fred was good-looking and bright, but he was very absent-minded. This was because his head was full of music. When he should have been thinking about his job, he was thinking of songs instead, and when he should have been working, he was playing on his flute.

If Bumberdumble Pott said to him, "Fred, throw out the rubbish and hang up my coat," Fred was just as likely to throw away the coat and hang up the rubbish.

In spite of this, Bumberdumble liked him and so did everyone else, because he was merry, kind, friendly, and always polite.

One day, Bumberdumble called together all the servants in the great hall of his house. Standing on the staircase where everyone could see and hear him, he said, "As you all know, I am the richest man in the land."

Everyone nodded. They knew.

"You might think I'd be very happy," Bumberdumble continued, "but I'm not. There is one thing I've wanted all my life, and that is the Bitter Fruit of Satisfaction. When I was young, I could have gone to find it but I was too busy making money. Now I am too old to make the journey. But if one of you will go and get it for me, I will give him half my wealth so that he will be as rich as I am."

Everyone thought that over. At last, the youngest of the butlers said, "Where is the Bitter Fruit of Satisfaction?"

Bumberdumble looked worried. "I am afraid it is a long way off," he admitted. "It is beyond six mountains and six sandy deserts, beyond the Boiling River and the Grimly Wood. And it is guarded by a Fire Drake."

"A Fire Drake? What's that? Something like a dragon?"

"Worse than a dragon," said Bumberdumble gloomily. "Much worse."

"Well," said the youngest of the butlers, "I can't go. I have to finish my job polishing the silver."

"I can't go," said the chief cook. "I have a wife and four children."

"I certainly can't go," said the oldest housemaid. "I have a sore knee."

And the more the others thought about the distance and the difficulties and the Fire Drake at the end of it, the more they thought of reasons why they couldn't go.

But finally, Fred said, "I'll go."

"You?" everyone cried.

"Why not?" said Fred, cheerfully. "I haven't any wife or children. I'm healthy, and you can always hire someone else to take over my jobs."

"But you'll forget where you're going before you've gone a kilometre," said the chief butler, with a chuckle.

"I will give him a map," said Bumberdumble. He came down the stairs and clapped Fred on the shoulder. "Bring me back the Bitter Fruit, my boy, and you will be richer than a king."

The next morning Fred set out. He had a knapsack full of food on his back, his flute in his pocket, a staff to lean on, and twenty gold pieces in his purse. He also had a map showing where the Bitter Fruit was, and Bumberdumble had hung this round his neck so he wouldn't forget to look at it.

Fred travelled for a whole, long year. He climbed six high rocky mountains, almost freezing at the tops of them. He tramped across six sandy deserts, almost dying of thirst. He crossed the Boiling River by going to its narrowest place and jumping from one slippery stone to another.

One evening, he came to an old dark house that stood on the edge of a vast dark wood. He was very weary, hungry, and tattered. His money had long ago been spent. He felt as if he could go no farther.

He knocked at the door, and it was opened by a pretty girl with blue eyes, black hair, and a smudge of dirt on her nose.

"Good evening," said Fred, politely, and then he dropped his staff and would have fallen, but the girl caught his arm and helped him into the house.

There was a bright fire burning and a good smell of cooking in the air.

The girl sat Fred down at the long table and put a bowl of soup in front of him. While he ate, she sat down opposite and watched him.

"You've come a long way," she said.

Fred told her who he was and where he was going. "And I have no idea how to take the Bitter Fruit when I find it," he said sadly, "or how I shall escape the Fire Drake. But if you will let me stay here until I'm rested, maybe I will think of something."

"This isn't my house," said the girl. "It belongs to the Witch of Grimly Wood. She's at a witchery meeting now, and while she's away you may certainly rest here and get your strength back. But when she returns, I don't know whether she'll let you stay, for she is the stingiest person in the world. Perhaps you can pay her in some way?"

"All I have is some music," said Fred. "What's your name?"

"Melissa," said the girl.

"Then I'll play you some special Melissa music, by way of thanks," said Fred.

He put the flute to his lips. His music was like the clear calling of summer birds at evening. Melissa listened and sighed. That night, Fred slept on the floor in front of the fire. The next day he rested and played his flute and told stories about his travels and made Melissa laugh. Working for a witch, she didn't get the chance to laugh very often. She was a good cook and fed him well, and she thought she had never liked anyone half so much.

The following morning, she said, "I am going to help you. I have three gifts my father gave me before he died, and I'll lend them to you. Maybe they will help you get the Bitter Fruit."

She brought out a pair of red slippers, a hat with a feather in it, and a sword.

"These," she said, "are the Shoes of Swiftness, the Cap of Darkness, and the Sword of Sharpness. The shoes will make you run swifter than an arrow, the cap will make you invisible, and the sword will cut through anything."

"Fine!" said Fred. "If I'm invisible, maybe I can steal the Bitter Fruit. If not, maybe I can kill the Fire Drake with the sword. And if that fails, I can run like anything."

At that moment they heard a noise outside.

"It's the witch," said Melissa. "Don't say a word to her about where you're going or how much Bumberdumble is going to pay you. She loves gold more than anything."

The door swung open. In came a puff of cold grey air, and with it the witch.

"Aha!" she croaked. "A stranger! Who are you, and what do you mean by sitting in my kitchen and eating my food?"

"My name is Fred," said Fred. And then, being absent-minded, he promptly forgot about Melissa's warning. "I'm on my way to get the Bitter Fruit of Satisfaction," he said. "When I take it back to Bumberdumble Pott, he will give me half his gold and I'll be richer than a king."

"Is that so?" said the witch. "I know where the Bitter Fruit is — it's just the other side of the Grimly Wood. I'll get it and give it to Bumberdumble Pott and collect the gold myself!" She spun round on her toe, jumped on her broomstick, and shot out of the room, slamming the door behind her.

"Quick!" cried Melissa. "The shoes!"

Fred pulled on the red slippers. He leaped up and off he ran. But not very far.

He had forgotten to open the door. *Thump*! He ran headfirst into it and knocked himself flat.

He struggled up, rubbing his head. "I told you I was absent-minded, didn't I?" he said.

"Never mind," said Melissa. "I'll show you a short cut. With the magic shoes, you can still get there first."

She led him outside and showed him a secret path among the trees. "This will take you straight through Grimly Wood," said she, "to a high hedge of thorns. On the other side of the hedge is the Bitter Fruit."

The Shoes of Swiftness carried Fred along the path like a flash of light from the eye of a lighthouse. At the high thorny hedge he drew the Sword of Sharpness. One-two, he slashed, and made a hole large enough to get through.

On the other side, there was a glass table.

On the table stood a silver tree with one small, dry, brown fruit hanging from it. And behind the table was the Fire Drake. It was scaly and slithery, bigger than a dragon and twice as fierce.

Fred snatched out the Cap of Darkness and put it on his head. But he was so busy looking at the Fire Drake that he wasn't thinking about what he was doing, and he put it on backwards. At once, everything disappeared. Everything but Fred. He couldn't see the Fire Drake or the glass table or the tree. He couldn't even see the ground. It looked as if he were standing on nothing in the middle of nothing.

But he could still feel the earth under his feet. In a panic, he dropped to his hands and knees.

It was the best thing he could have done, for at the same instant the Fire Drake blew out a sheet of flame. It would have crisped Fred up like a piece of burnt toast if it had touched him, but it went right over him.

"Oh," he groaned. "If only I weren't so absent-minded."

He reached up and turned the Cap of Darkness round on his head. Now he could see everything again, but *he* was invisible. He got shakily to his feet. He could see the Fire Drake looking this way and that in puzzlement. He tiptoed over to the silver tree.

The fruit was gone.

He understood what had happened. While the Fire Drake had been shooting its flames at him, the witch had sneaked up and stolen the fruit.

Fred ran back through the Grimly Wood to the witch's house. There was the witch, just packing her suitcase for the long broomstick flight to Bumberdumble's house.

"Stop!" yelled Fred.

With one chop of the Sword of Sharpness he cut her broomstick in two.

The witch snatched a handful of ashes from the fire and threw them into the air. They settled over Fred and then she could see him, like a faint grey shadow.

"So it's you, miserable wretch!" she screamed. "I'll
turn you into a piece of waste paper and throw you away."
She began to mumble a wicked spell.
"Stop her!" cried Melissa. "Use your sword!"
Fred lifted the sword. Then he lowered it again. "I can't,"
he said. "It wouldn't be polite."

The witch raised her hands. The spell was ready.

"Then cut the ground out from under her," snapped Melissa.

Fred whirled the sword. He sliced away the floor under the witch's feet. Down she fell.

Under the floor there was a bottomless well. The witch fell into it and that was the end of her.

Fred removed the Cap of Darkness and dusted himself off He handed the cap, the shoes, and the sword to Melissa.

"Thank you," he said. "But do you know, I forgot something."

"What?"

"The Bitter Fruit of Satisfaction. I forgot that the witch was holding it. She is still holding it, wherever she is."

"What a shame," said Melissa.

Fred scratched his head.

"Oh, I don't know," he said. "If you will marry me, I would really rather have you than be richer than a king."

So they settled down in the witch's house — after fixing the hole in the floor — and they were happy together. And since Fred could play as much music as he liked whenever he liked, he was never absent-minded again except once in a while.

As for Bumberdumble Pott, if he never got the Bitter Fruit, at any rate he remained the richest man in the land, and that was better than nothing.

Jay Williams
Illustrated by Terry Denton

FRIENDS

Friends share

ice creams and comics and potato chips,

wish bones and gum and camping trips,

monopoly games and each other's clothes,

but most of all secrets that no one else knows.

Secrets

like being afraid of the dentist's chair,

or arriving home when no one's there;

like being scared when the teacher yells,

or being caught out when somebody tells;

like wanting to cry when the story is sad,

or words you whisper when really mad.

Friends share

all these things and hundreds more.

That's what they're for.

The painting is by
Rie Muñoz, who lives
in Juneau, Alaska.
The poem is by
Pat Edwards who lives
in Sydney.
Both the painting and
the poem are called
"Friends".

Secret words

Glossary

"amkneesyer" (*p. 59*)
she meant "amnesia" which is when you lose your memory

awesome (*p. 15*)
something that fills you with a mix of fear and respect

bandicoots (*p. 23*)
large burrowing rats

canopy (*p. 21*)
large wide covering (here, of trees)

chafe (*p. 20*)
rubbing

cloying (*p. 46*)
they stuck to his body

commotion (*p. 72*)
confused noise

contemptible (*p. 11*)
someone you can't respect

courteous (*p. 69*)
polite and considerate

deference to (*p. 33*)
respect for

ermine (*p. 70*)
white fur from stoats that live in northern regions: they have a white winter coat with a black-tipped tail

fatiguing (*p. 75*)
tiring

gelding (*p. 19*)
a castrated male horse

glowered (*p. 48*)
looked angrily

Great Barrier Reef (*p. 21*)
a coral reef off the north-east coast of Australia — the largest coral reef in the world

haughty (*p. 70*)
full of self-importance

on his haunches (*p. 43*)
it means he crouched down low

humiliation (*p. 49*)
when your pride is hurt and you are made to feel small

keenly (*p. 72*)
with interest

Glossary continues on page 96

lantana (*p. 20*)
a shrub with spikes of yellow or orange flowers

manta ray (*p. 21*)
a large, flat fish

pied (*p. 72*)
with markings of two or more colours

profuse (*p. 44*)
plentiful

quavered (*p. 32*)
said in a trembling voice

scabbard (*p. 71*)
holder for a sword

sleek (*p. 43*)
shiny; healthy

sneer (*p. 75*)
an expression of scorn

stern (*p. 20*)
strict

strident (*p. 49*)
loud and harsh

suckle (*p. 43*)
give milk to

switch (*p. 20*)
a flexible rod or twig

taut (*p. 20*)
tightly stretched

tormentors (*p. 22*)
people or things that worry and annoy

ungainly (*p. 70*)
awkward looking

vow (*p. 12*)
make a solemn and binding promise

what ailed me (*p. 15*)
what troubled me